DEFENSE, SECURITY AND STRATEGIES

SEXUAL ASSAULT PREVENTION BY THE DEPARTMENT OF DEFENSE

STRATEGY AND ASSESSMENT

DEFENSE, SECURITY AND STRATEGIES

Additional books in this series can be found on Nova's website under the Series tab.

Additional e-books in this series can be found on Nova's website under the eBooks tab.

CONTENTS

PREFACE

Sexual assault is a crime that devastates victims and has a far-reaching negative impact for The Department of Defense (DOD) because it undermines DOD's core values, degrades mission readiness, and raises financial costs. DOD developed its strategy to prevent sexual assault using the Centers for Disease Control and Prevention (CDC) framework for effective sexual-violence prevention strategies, but DOD does not link activities to desired outcomes or fully identify risk and protective factors. This book addresses the extent to which DOD developed an effective prevention strategy; implemented activities department-wide and at military installations related to the department's effort to prevent sexual assault; and developed performance measures to determine the effectiveness of its efforts to prevent sexual assault in the military.

In: Sexual Assault Prevention … ISBN: 978-1-63485-351-4
Editor: Jonathan Maldonado

Chapter 1

2014-2016 Sexual Assault Prevention Strategy*

Department of Defense

SECRETARY OF DEFENSE
1000 DEFENSE PENTAGON
WASHINGTON, DC 20301-1000

MAY 0 1 2014

MEMORANDUM FOR SECRETARIES OF THE MILITARY DEPARTMENTS
CHAIRMAN OF THE JOINT CHIEFS OF STAFF
UNDER SECRETARY OF DEFENSE FOR PERSONNEL AND READINESS
CHIEFS OF THE MILITARY SERVICES
CHIEF OF THE NATIONAL GUARD BUREAU
GENERAL COUNSEL OF THE DEPARTMENT OF DEFENSE

SUBJECT: Sexual Assault Prevention and Response

As leaders of the Department of Defense, we share a commitment to ensuring the safety and welfare of our people as well as the health of this institution and the trust of the American people. Our collaborative efforts to combat sexual assault are making a difference in the choices of victims who are seeking care and reporting in unprecedented numbers. Still, we must continue to sustain our commitment to developing and employing essential reforms to enhance the administration of military justice, increase accountability, and ensure a healthy and respectful command climate throughout the Armed Forces. As we work together to overcome underreporting of this crime, it is essential that victims have confidence in our accountability and response systems.

* This is an edited, reformatted and augmented version of a Document issued April 2014.

In the past year, we have all taken aggressive action to improve victim confidence, including the creation of dedicated legal support to victims, enhanced access to victim advocacy, and increased training and awareness for the entire force. Furthermore, we are working to implement the most sweeping reforms to the Uniform Code of Military Justice since 1968. We will continue to engage victims to ensure their voices are heard and to field responsive services to the men and women who suffer the terrible wounds of this crime. As seen in the Fiscal Year (FY) 2013 Annual Report on Sexual Assault in the Military, more victims are reporting this crime and accessing support. The FY13 Annual Report, however, clearly demonstrates a persistent problem and an urgent need to step up our efforts to prevent this crime.

Preventing sexual assault in the military requires a personal commitment from all Service members, at every level, to be a steadfast participant in creating an appropriate culture and upholding standards of behavior and military core values. We can and will address the entire continuum of harm by embedding prevention principles throughout the Department and underscoring the importance of individual actions to establish an environment of dignity and respect. Ultimately, we must ensure that every Service member understands that sexist behaviors, sexual harassment, and sexual assault are not tolerated, condoned, or ignored. Every Service member must live our values and possess the social courage to act to reduce risk, safely and proactively intervene to stop inappropriate behavior and to report crimes.

Therefore, I am directing the implementation of the attached 2014-2016 DoD Sexual Assault Prevention Strategy, which through a collaborative Department-wide approach, provides authoritative guidance on delivering consistent and effective prevention methods and programs. This plan builds on your efforts and identifies leaders at all levels as critical components in prevention and integrates accountability, community involvement, communication, deterrence, incentives, training, education, and harm reduction. The Secretaries of the Military Departments, with input from the Chiefs of the Military Services, and Chief of the National Guard Bureau (NGB) will report back to me on implementation of this strategy by July 31, 2014, with a copy to the Under Secretary of Defense for Personnel and Readiness (USD(P&R)).

In addition, I am directing immediate implementation of the following measures to further strengthen our shared approach to sexual assault prevention programs:

- ***Advance and Sustain Appropriate Culture:*** To further enhance prevention programs, the Secretaries of the Military Departments, in conjunction with the Chiefs of the Military Services and NGB, will update and integrate gender-responsive and culturally competent programs for leaders and Service members to address healthy relationships, active bystander intervention, social courage, and core values that support the establishment of mutual respect. In addition, the Chiefs of Military Services will review policies that influence culture and behavior on military installations and in units, and adjust policy within their purview, as appropriate. Report your implementation plans and methods, and recommendations to me through the USD(P&R) by November 1, 2014.

- ***Evaluate Commander SAPR Training:*** To ensure that all leaders are educated on sexual assault response policies and provided the appropriate tools to prevent the crime, the USD(P&R) will conduct assessments of the effectiveness of newly-developed core competencies and learning objectives for Pre-Command and Senior Enlisted Leader Sexual Assault Prevention and Response (SAPR) training. USD(P&R) will report findings to me by September 1, 2014.

- ***Review Alcohol Policies:*** To improve safety and reduce the risks posed by alcohol, the Secretaries of the Military Departments will review and as necessary revise alcohol policies to address risk factors beyond the individual use of alcohol, to include such matters as training of alcohol providers, emphasizing responsible sales practices, and engaging local community leadership and organizations to expand efforts off-post. Report your implementation plan and methods to me through the USD(P&R) by November 1, 2014.

- ***Improve Reporting for Male Victims:*** To promote recovery among male victims, the Secretaries of the Military Departments, in conjunction with Chiefs of the Military Services and NGB, will implement and monitor methods to improve reporting and enhance efforts to encourage male victims to seek assistance. Solicit male victim input in the development of these methods. Report your implementation plan and methods to me through the USD(P&R) by January 5, 2015.

- ***Develop Collaborative Forum for Sexual Assault Prevention Methods:*** To leverage and advance ongoing research and effective preventative methods, the USD(P&R) will establish a community of practice and collaboration forum to share best and promising practices and lessons learned with external experts, federal partners, Military Services, NGB advocacy organizations, and educational institutions. USD(P&R) will report the implementation plan and methods to me by August 1, 2014.

- ***Develop Standardized and Voluntary Survey for Victims/Survivors:*** To further improve our collective response by engaging victims, the Chiefs of the Military Services and NGB, in cooperation with the USD(P&R), will jointly develop and participate in a standardized victim survey. This survey tool will provide the sexual assault victim/survivor the opportunity to provide feedback on their experiences with SAPR victim assistance, the military health system, the military justice process, and other areas of support. The survey shall be developed collaboratively and regularly administered in such a way that protects victim privacy and does not impact adversely victim legal and health status. The USD(P&R) will report the joint methods and implementation plan to me no later than June 1, 2014.

Considerable efforts are underway to combat sexual assault. Our success depends on a continued proactive, focused, and comprehensive approach. Our mission can only be accomplished when everyone understands their role in preventing this crime. Your strong leadership has been and will continue to be essential in our prevention efforts as the words and actions of leaders set the tone of dignity and respect. If leaders establish the right climate, Service members will be clear on what they need to do to prevent sexual assault and victims will feel more confident in accessing support. These initiatives and plans, in addition to our ongoing efforts, provide a roadmap for this Department to enable military readiness, establish an enduring culture of dignity and respect, and eliminate this crime from our military.

Thank you.

Chuck Hagel

Attachment:
As stated

cc:
Under Secretaries of Defense
Commanders of the Combatant Commands
Inspector General of the Department of Defense
Assistant Secretaries of Defense
Directors of the Defense Agencies
Directors of the DoD Field Activities

Foreword

Leaders of the Department of Defense,

Eliminating sexual assault from the military is one of the Department of Defense's highest priorities. We share a commitment to ensuring the safety and welfare of our people as well as the health of this institution and the trust of the American people. Preventing sexual assault in the military requires a personal commitment from every Service member, at every level, to be a steadfast participant in creating an appropriate culture, upholding standards of behavior, and advancing our shared core values. Many of you have already taken great strides to prevent this crime. However, our mutual success depends on a shared, proactive, comprehensive approach that empowers everyone to act in an environment shaped to promote the best possible outcomes.

Our prevention strategy recognizes that true prevention is much more than an annual training or weekend safety briefings. Rather, our approach must involve a wide range of integrated elements addressing policy, accountability, community involvement, communication, deterrence, incentives, and harm reduction. Within the United States Armed Forces, leaders at all levels are the "center of gravity" that can leverage these many elements as we grow our climate of dignity and respect.

This past year, our Service members heard the words of their leadership, believed our expressed commitment to care for victims, and reported allegations of sexual assault in record numbers. Although we have made progress in our response to this crime, we still have much work to do before we are able to confidently say that this problem has been erased from our ranks. I have full faith and confidence in our abilities and leadership as we strive to reduce and ultimately eliminate sexual assault from the military.

Thank you,

Chuck Hagel
Secretary of Defense

1. Introduction

The uniformed leadership communicated its resolve to prevent sexual assault with its Strategic Direction to the Joint Force, published in May 2012. In it, the members of the Joint Chiefs of Staff provided their collective guidance to the U.S. Armed Forces and described the importance of prevention:

> "Prevention is the most critical Line of Effort (LOE); it ultimately defines program success. Unlike the other LOEs, prevention has neither a beginning nor an end. It informs and is informed by the other LOEs. There are tangible aspects of prevention that promote a positive command

climate/environment including program training and education. However, there are also intangible aspects that translate education and training to promote a professional culture that imbues knowledge, awareness, communication, personal responsibility and the empowerment to act".[1]

Following the guidance outlined by the Secretary of Defense in the 2013 Department of Defense (DoD) Sexual Assault Prevention and Response Strategic Plan, the Sexual Assault Prevention and Response Office (SAPRO) developed and executed a sexual assault prevention campaign to identify evidence-based prevention practices and lessons learned, in order to update the *2008 Department of Defense Sexual Assault Prevention Strategy*. This plan was created through collaboration between DoD SAPRO, the Military Services, and other SAPR stakeholders. The revised *2014-2016 DoD Sexual Assault Prevention Strategy* continues this effort to establish a central plan.

The objectives of this plan are to achieve unity of effort and purpose across all of DoD in the execution of sexual assault prevention, to develop objective criteria for measuring progress, and to publish tasks that operationalize the Prevention LOE. This plan will continue to be a dynamic document and reviewed every two years. This plan will be managed and updated by USD (P&R) through DoD SAPRO, in coordination with the Military Departments and Services, and the National Guard Bureau, using existing oversight mechanisms, and the responsive input of collective stakeholders.

DoD capabilities employed in support of this plan are assigned the Office of the Secretary of Defense, the Chairman of the Joint Chiefs of Staff, the Joint Staff, the Combatant Commands, the Military Departments, and the National Guard Bureau. This strategic approach will guide and inform policy development, organization, training, and employment of the variety of means used to operationalize this strategy. Stakeholders include:

- Office of the Secretary of Defense (OSD) – Sexual Assault Prevention and Response Office (SAPRO), Office of the Deputy Assistant Secretary of Defense for Military Personnel Policy (DASD/MPP), Office of the Deputy Assistant Secretary of Defense for Civilian Personnel Policy (DASD/CPP), Office of Legal Policy (OLP); Legislative Affairs (OSD LA); Public Affairs (OSD PA); Deputy Assistant Secretary of Defense for Readiness (DASD(R)), Office of DoD General Counsel (OGC), Assistant Secretary of Defense, Health Affairs (HA), Office of the Deputy Assistant Secretary of Defense for

Military Community and Family Policy (DASD/MC&FP), Office of Diversity Management and Equal Opportunity (ODMEO), the Defense Manpower Data Center (DMDC), the Defense Equal Opportunity Management Institute (DEOMI), and Deputy Assistant Secretary of Defense for Reserve Affairs (DASD/RA).

- The Joint Chiefs of Staff (JCS)
- The Military Departments – Departments of the Army, Navy, and Air Force
- The Military Services – The Army, Navy, Air Force, and Marine Corps
- The National Guard Bureau (NGB)

This plan is not all encompassing or fully exhaustive of all sexual assault prevention activities performed within or by the DoD community. Instead, this plan highlights and captures resources, methods and tasks that directly contribute to the strategic objectives set forth in this document, as identified by plan stakeholders.

1.1. Relationship to Directives and Instructions

In this strategic construct, policy issuances promulgated by the DoD function as tools employed by sexual assault prevention and response elements. The promulgation of policy in accordance with these tasks further operationalizes the strategy approach outlined in the *DoD Sexual Assault Prevention Strategy*. DoD Components and the Secretaries of the Military Departments will align implementing plans and policies with this Strategy.

Overall, *DoD Directive 6495.01, Sexual Assault Prevention and Response Program*, establishes DoD policy and assigns responsibilities for prevention, advocacy, and victim care. *DoD Instruction 6495.02, SAPR Program Procedures, and associated Service policies,* further operationalize this program.

1.2. Defining Prevention

In an effort to establish shared understandings of prevention, DoD adopted the U.S. Centers for Disease Control and Prevention (CDC) definition of prevention as it applies to sexual violence. The CDC identifies three levels of prevention based on when the prevention efforts occur:

- Primary Prevention: Approaches that take place before sexual violence has occurred to prevent initial perpetration.
- Secondary Prevention: Immediate responses after sexual violence has occurred to address the early identification of victims and the short-term consequences of violence.
- Tertiary Prevention: Long-term responses after sexual violence has occurred to address the lasting consequences of violence and sex offender treatment interventions.

Primary prevention is characterized as;

> "Population-based and/or environmental and system-level strategies, policies, and actions that prevent sexual violence from initially occurring. Such prevention efforts work to modify and/or entirely eliminate the events, conditions, situations, or exposure to influences (risk factors) that result in the initiation of sexual violence and associated injuries, disabilities, and deaths".[2]

CDC also distinguishes between prevention strategies based upon the group for whom the intervention is intended. Using this type of differentiation, sexual violence interventions can again be divided into three categories:

- Universal Interventions: Approaches that are aimed at groups or the general population regardless of individual risk for sexual violence perpetration or victimization.
- Selected Interventions: Approaches that are aimed at those who are thought to have a *heightened risk* for sexual violence perpetration or victimization.
- Indicated Interventions: Approaches that are aimed at those who have already *perpetrated* sexual violence or have been *victimized.*[3]

DoD places primary prevention at the core of its focus in developing prevention-related tasks and initiatives which seek to reduce, with the goal to eliminate, the factors leading to, or associated with, sexual violence, thereby stopping the crime before it occurs. Hence, prevention programs **will not** rely solely on training and education of individuals considered to be at risk and/or harm reduction activities (formerly risk reduction). Primary prevention involves empowered and competent individuals interacting in an environment that has been sustained to promote the best possible outcomes.

1.3. Defining the Sexual Assault Threat and Environment

Although the Department has made great strides in sexual assault prevention and response in recent years, research suggests that sexual assault remains a significant problem in the Armed Forces. As in the civilian sector and contrary to common perception, most sexual assaults are perpetrated by someone known to the victim. While some sexual assaults are perpetrated by strangers in attacks that leave the victim visibly injured, most crimes are perpetrated between people who know each other, often facilitated by alcohol (weapon of choice), and limited to few visible injuries. This non-stranger fact pattern has a number of significant implications for prevention efforts, particularly given that most people believe the stranger fact pattern often depicted in popular culture. The results of the *2012 Workplace and Gender Relations Survey of Active Duty Members (*WGRA) showed that sexual harassment and stalking are related with perpetration of sexual assaults; 58% of women and 42% of men surveyed who reported having been sexually assaulted also received some form of sexual harassment and/or stalking by the alleged offender, prior to, or after the unwanted sexual contact incident. (see ***Figure 1*** below).

Unwanted sexual contact incidents characteristics for 2012		Women	Men
Alcohol/Drug Involvement	You or the offender had been drinking alcohol before the incident	47%	19%
	You or the offender had been using drugs before the incident	2%	8%
	Offender used drugs to knock you out	3%	9%
Use of Threats/Force	Use some degree of physical force (e.g., holding you down)	50%	22%
	Threaten to ruin your reputation if you did not consent	17%	21%
	Threaten to physically harm you if you did not consent	12%	18%
Sexual Harassment/Stalking by Offender Before/After the Assault	Sexually harassed you only	30%	19%
	Stalked you only	8%	2%
	Both sexually harassed and stalked you	20%	21%
	Neither sexually harassed nor stalked you	42%	58%

Figure 1.

Reporting, Societal Influences, and Military Challenges

Effective sexual assault prevention requires an understanding of the problem and the environment in which sexual assaults occur. Since 2006, Department research has found that, of those surveyed, between 4.4% and 6.8% of active duty women and between 0.9% and 1.8% of active duty men indicate experiencing unwanted sexual contact in the year prior to being surveyed.[4] In addition, a substantial percentage of women and men taking the 2012 WGRA indicated experiencing unwanted sexual contact prior to entering the military and/or at some time during their military career.[5] However, sexual assaults continue to be underreported, meaning that each year the number of sexual assault victims reported to DoD authorities is lower than the number of sexual assaults estimated to occur. Underreporting makes it more difficult for alleged offenders to be identified so that they can be held appropriately accountable. Civilian and military research shows that one significant barrier to reporting is concern by victims over how they will be perceived by others. Such perceptions are primed by common attitudes towards sexual assault victims in our society, such as acceptance of rape myths, victim blaming, and reluctance to become involved, that are evident throughout our culture. Widespread objectification of men and women in the media can reinforce these attitudes. Those who view sex as an act of competition or conquest (e.g., "scoring") further normalize attitudes and behaviors that perpetuate sexual violence. Countering these widely prevalent perceptions requires a consistent messaging campaign that promotes our military culture as an environment of dignity and respect.

There are barriers to reporting the crime of sexual assault. First, there is a perceived stigma associated with reporting sexual assaults in an environment that idealizes confidence, decisiveness, and strength. Thus, military members are particularly impacted by this stigma, as many are concerned about being mislabeled as weak or experiencing inappropriate scrutiny of their sexual orientation. Second, the hierarchical nature of the military presents the opportunity to employ sexual coercion to obtain gratification from subordinates. Third, research indicates most sexual assault victims fear being blamed for the crime. Victim blaming often occurs when confidentiality is breached and the private lives of victims, including their behaviors immediately leading up to the crime, are scrutinized. Even with the protections afforded certain communications in both policy and law, maintaining confidentiality in the military environment is difficult. Given the close knit military environment, information about a sexual assault may spread and polarize units. As a result, command teams are faced with an urgent and important role in maintaining focus on mission execution, readiness, and morale.

Role of Alcohol

While many sexual assaults occur without the involvement of alcohol, alcohol adversely affects decision-making and impulse control.[6] Alcohol degrades one's ability to identify and counter threats in the environment, which may impair the response of those bystanders that could assist an intended victim or deter a potential offender. Effective prevention also requires an understanding of the role alcohol plays in the perpetration of sexual violence. In addition, alcohol may be used by the alleged offender as a weapon to reduce a victim's resistance or fully incapacitate a victim.

Leaders' Role in Reducing the Risk of Sexual Assault

Military-specific research highlights the contribution that a hostile work environment has on sexual assault. Military research identifies several factors that significantly increase the likelihood of sexual assault within a unit: if the climate is one that is hostile to women (e.g., demeaning, objectifying), the risk of sexual assault increases by six times; officers initiating or allowing demeaning comments or gestures toward women increases the risk of sexual assault by five times.[7] The conclusion of this and other research is that there is a strong positive correlation between the frequency of sexual harassment in a military unit and sexual assault within the unit.[8]

Leaders are responsible for creating climates of mutual respect and diginity. To help leaders better understand the factors at play within their units, the Department updated the sexual assault prevention and response questions on the DEOMI Equal Opportunity Climate Survey to better assist commanders to identify damaging attitudes and behaviors within their units. Conducting a climate assessment enhances a leader's knowledge about the specific needs of his or her unit or organization. Commanders must then use this unit-specific information to develop their approach to sexual assault response and prevention. To this end, leaders must employ targeted interventions, standards, and messaging to address issues unique to their unit climate. While prevention programs may draw upon common themes, strategies and messages should be tailored to specific audiences and for specific purposes and circumstances. Prevention messaging and initiatives must:

- Help Service members recognize and mitigate risk factors associated with sexual assault and **influence** them to promote protective factors, intervene safely, and support victims;
- **Deter** Service members from engaging in inappropriate or illegal behaviors inconsistent with our military values; and
- **Identify** those few who commit sexual assaults so they can be held appropriately accountable. For more information, see **Appendix B: Defining the Threat and Environment Continued**.

1.4. Department of Defense Sexual Assault Prevention and Response Strategic Plan Overview

Five SAPR Lines of Effort (LOE) were established in the *2013 DoD SAPR Strategic Plan* to guide and focus strategic planning efforts with corresponding objectives and end states. The LOEs are Prevention, Investigation, Accountability, Advocacy/Victim Assistance, and Assessment. DoD Components use these LOEs as the foundational basis for their plans, to ensure unity of effort, synchronization, and the creation of a common approach to assessments. ***Figure 2*** depicts all the LOEs within the multi-pronged strategy. Using the prevention objective and end state outlined in this strategic plan as a baseline, DoD is expanding and providing additional guidance for the Prevention LOE through this revised *2014-2016 Sexual Assault Prevention Strategy*.

1.5. Planning Approach

To better understand the environment in which sexual assaults occur, DoD used CDC's social ecological model (SEM) ***Figure 3*** to establish a framework for understanding risk and protective factors, their influences, and their relationship to one another.

Risk factors increase the likelihood that sexual violence will occur. However, risk factors are not direct causes of sexual violence, but rather, contribute to an environment in which sexual violence is more likely. For example, a unit or command where women are objectified or demeaned or inappropriate comments about race or sexual orientation go uncorrected, may be perceived by some that they may get away with other acts against women or men, including sexual assault.

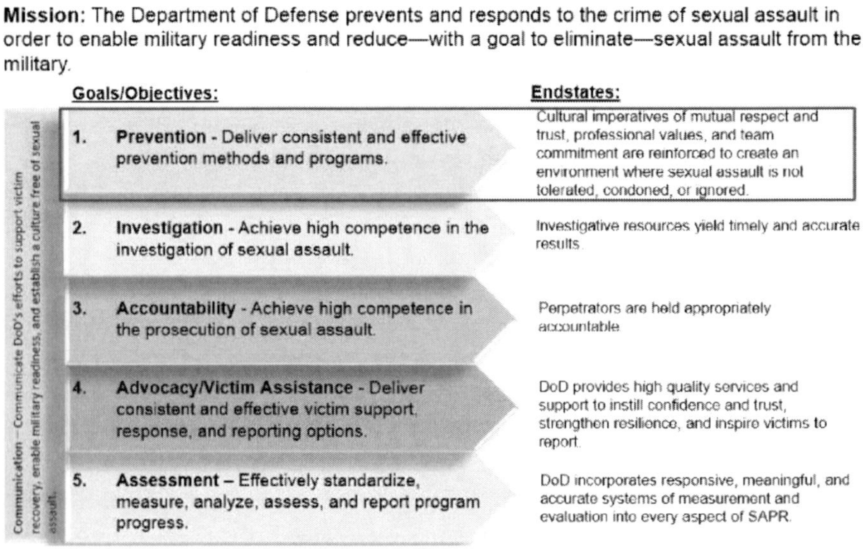

Figure 2.

Protective factors decrease the likelihood that sexual violence will occur, or buffer someone from becoming a victim or perpetrator of sexual violence. For example, the presence or actions taken by a trusted friend may interfere with or deter a potential offender's attempts to isolate and sexually assault an intended victim. For more information, see **Appendix C: Sexual Violence Risk and Protective Factors.**

The SEM model describes how each level of society has its own collection of risk factors and protective factors that must be considered when trying to achieve the prevention of sexual violence:

- **Individual-level influences** involve biological factors, personal history, and individual characteristics that increase or decrease the likelihood that an individual will become a victim or perpetrator of violence.
- **Interpersonal relationship-level influences** are factors that involve the interactions of peers, intimate partners, and family members.
- **Community-level influences** are factors at play in community and social environments and include an individual's experiences and relationships with schools, workplaces, and neighborhoods.
- **Societal-level influences** are larger, macro-level risk and protective factors that influence sexual violence such as gender inequality,

religious or cultural belief systems, societal norms, and economic or social policies that create or sustain gaps and tensions between groups of people.[9]

This model reemphasizes the understanding that prevention is not a single program or initiative. Rather, the model identifies multiple levels of interconnected influences across the society. This means that prevention efforts must occur at each level of society to have an impact. Furthermore, the social ecological model:

- Emphasizes the interwoven relationships that exist between individuals and their environment;
- Stresses that interventions at multiple levels are more likely to have a lasting effect than any single intervention; and
- Remains the predominant model for organizing prevention programs.

This model is utilized world-wide by leaders in public health and safety to combat HIV-AIDS, tobacco abuse, youth violence, and cancer.

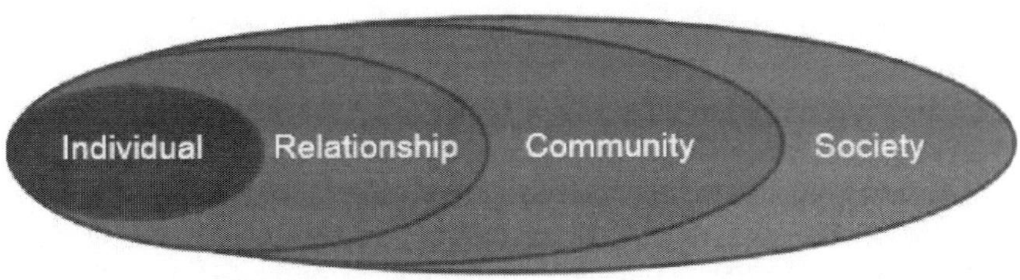

Figure 3.

Regardless of environment (DoD or civilian community), preventing sexual assault requires understanding and addressing the multiple risk and protective factors that influence its occurrence. Successful modification of these factors requires attention to both the individual and the environment. SAPRO adapted the CDC SEM model to address the unique nature of the military environment. Using operational art, described in Chapter III of Joint Operations Planning 5.0, SAPRO linked ends, ways, and means to achieve the desired end state.

2. Department of Defense Prevention Strategy Vision and Mission Statement

Vision: Our vision is a military environment where:

Every man and woman serving in the military lives and operates in a climate of mutual respect, free from sexual violence;

- Service members are motivated and empowered to intervene against inappropriate behaviors inconsistent with our core values;
- Effective sexual assault prevention practices are institutionalized across the Department of Defense; and The Department of Defense serves as a national leader in preventing sexual violence.

Mission: The DoD executes proactive and comprehensive sexual assault prevention programs in order to enable military readiness and reduce ‒with a goal to eliminate‒ sexual assault from the military.

3. Department of Defense Sexual Assault Prevention Model

Individuals within the DoD come from a wide variety of backgrounds and their past experiences shape their attitudes and behavior in response to life events. Individuals may express themselves in different ways, and for some, violence may be a choice. At the core of the model ***Figure 4*** is the Individual, surrounded by four interconnected spheres of influence representing Relationships (e.g., family, friends, peers, coworkers), Leaders at all levels, DoD/Services/Units (the organizations that constitute "the military community"), and Society (includes popular culture). Recognizing the essential role of leadership, DoD included leaders as a distinct sphere of influence to highlight the necessity that commanders and their staffs develop and execute tactics that target this "center of gravity" for prevention efforts. Due to the complex nature of the problem, it is important to conduct a number of interventions (actions) that span multiple levels to achieve the greatest, lasting impact.

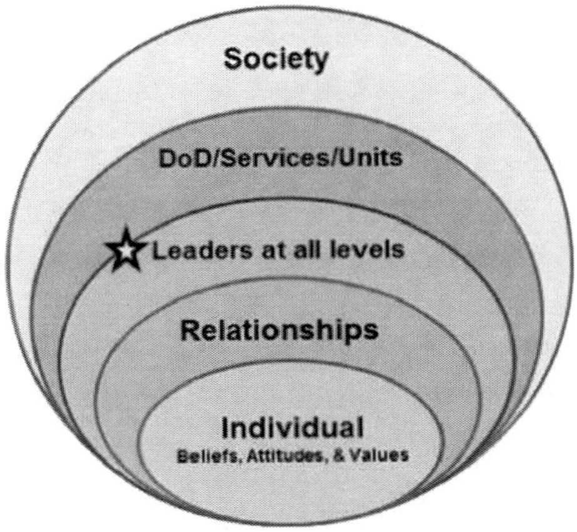

Figure 4.

4. Department of Defense Prevention Strategy

As depicted in ***Figure 5***, the 2014-2016 Sexual Assault Prevention Strategy is a proactive and comprehensive approach to prevent sexual assault on multiple levels. The key objectives of the strategy are to inform public policy and legislation (Society); institutionalize prevention practices and programs across the force (DoD/Service/Unit); set and enforce standards for appropriate conduct and integrating prevention into command practices (Leaders at all levels); mentor, develop skills, and educate Service members to promote healthy relationships and intervene against inappropriate or unacceptable behaviors (Relationships/Individuals).

For several years, our primary prevention efforts were focused on conducting SAPR training and education (Individual/Relationships). This updated prevention strategy shifts the emphasis to enhancing DoD/Service and Leader's capabilities. This will ensure that leaders are prepared to establish a climate that supports sexual assault prevention while placing renewed emphasis on institutionalizing sexual assault prevention policies and practices. The strategy provides a framework (spheres of influence), means (resources), ways (methods), and supporting end states to assist leaders and planners in the development of appropriate tasks (see Appendix A for tasks).

Prevention messaging designed to influence, deter, and detect

Spheres of Influence	*Means* (Resources)	*Ways* (Methods)	Supporting *End states*
Society	• DoD Benchmark Prevention Programs and Research • Community Volunteers • Collaboration with federal partners, coalitions, and other primary prevention experts	• Inform public policies and legislation that support primary prevention of sexual assault • Inform and Influence cultural belief system to discourage sexual assault and support victims • Develop DoD national benchmark prevention program that sets the example for civil society to follow	Acceptance and endorsement of the values shared by DoD which seek to prevent sexual assault
DoD/Services/ Units	• Service Values • Directives and Strategies • Policies & Guides • Military Law (UCMJ) • Accountability & Monitoring • Prevention Tools • Info. sharing & Collaboration Forums	• Institutionalize sexual assault prevention practices and programs throughout Department • Ensure enduring Department-wide focus and attention to the critical role SAPR issues play in mission accomplishment and readiness • Provide support and resources to leaders for preventing and responding to sexual assault	Institutionalized culture & values, supported by policies, which recognizes and emphasizes the importance of preventing sexual assault
Leaders at all levels	• Leader mentorship (formal/informal) • Unit climate • Guidance & local policies • Monitoring, deterrence, and accountability measures and strategies • Networks	• Influence personnel values, attitudes, and behaviors • Set and enforce standards for appropriate conduct • Integrate sexual assault prevention into unit practices at the strategic, operational, and tactical levels • Implement policies to increase protective factors and reduce risk factors • Detection, deterrence, and accountability of inappropriate behaviors within the unit	Establishment and maintenance of a culture/climate which supports the prevention of sexual assault
Relationships	Education, skills building and training on personal responsibility, empathy, healthy relationships, military core values, and bystander intervention	• Promote healthy and supportive relationships between peers, partners, family, and friends • Promote pro-active intervention in inter-personal harassment and violence incidents	An environment in which Service members' networks support a culture of sexual assault prevention
Individuals	Education, skills building and training on personal responsibility, empathy, healthy relationships, military core values, and bystander intervention	• Promote healthy social-emotional relationship skills • Engage all personnel to address interpersonal violence in their community • Promote empathy • Acknowledge personal responsibility for acceptable behavior and model conduct	Identify, act, and intervene to prevent inappropriate behavior of any kind including sexual harassment and assault

Figure 5.

5. Successful Military Prevention Program Elements

To address all the spheres of influence and reach the Strategy supporting end states (Figure 5), prevention programs should integrate a variety of practices using a comprehensive approach. Single-faceted (e.g., Training only or Deterrence only) efforts have not shown long term effectiveness in reducing sexual assault. DoD SAPRO researched promising practices[10] and developed the following recommended list of elements to include in all sexual assault prevention programs:

➢ Leadership Involvement at all Levels **(Center of Gravity)**

Leaders at all levels are the center of gravity for the prevention of sexual assault. Leaders are responsible for the climate of their unit and the welfare of their subordinates. The leader also assembles the resources with the requisite skills and expertise for a successful SAPR program. If the leader is successful in establishing a climate of safety and trust, members may feel more comfortable coming forward with issues and reports of incidents. Examples include:

- Providing mentorship, setting the example of appropriate behavior for others to model, and quickly correcting those who engage in sexually harassing or sexist behaviors;
- Continually focus on sustaining a healthy command climate and enforcing of standards;
- Providing vision and guidance for the execution of the sexual assault prevention program;
- Delivering appropriate sexual assault prevention and response messages to their unit;
- Setting expectations regarding accountability for behavior and offenses; and
- Ensuring new members have a sponsor in the unit.

➢ Peer to Peer Mentorship (informal leaders)

Promoting healthy relationships between peers, partners, family, and friends has shown promise to enhance a healthy command climate and prevent sexual assault. Peer mentors can integrate relevant values, attitudes, and behaviors related to sexual assault prevention reinforcing our core military values and professional standards. Examples of relevant topics peers can promote include:

- Victim empathy;
- Bystander intervention against any unacceptable behavior;
- Healthy relationships;
- Moderate, responsible alcohol use; and
- Obtaining consent for sexual activity.

➢ **Accountability**

When all personnel are held appropriately accountable for their behavior, the unit climate of trust and safety is enhanced and personnel may feel safer coming forward with issues or incident reports. At the same time, senior commanders must hold subordinate commanders appropriately accountable for supporting and maintaining a unit command climate that promotes respect, tolerance, and diversity, and not one that tolerates sexual harassment, discrimination or sexual assault. Examples of practices that promote accountability include:

- Publicizing the punishments for misconduct or criminal offenses consistent with law and Department of Defense regulations;
- Incorporating SAPR monitoring into readiness assessments (e.g., quarterly training briefings, operational readiness assessments, inspections) to ensure program implementation and compliance;
- Senior leadership engaging with subordinate commands to review results and progress with command climate assessments; and
- Ensuring all allegations of sexual assault are referred to Military Criminal Investigative Organizations (MCIOs).

➢ **Organizational Support (Resources)**

The Department of Defense must institutionalize sexual assault prevention programs. The necessary resources include:

- Manpower;
- Budget;
- Tools and systems;
- Policies;
- Education and training;
- Standard operating procedures; and
- Continuous evaluation and improvement.

➢ **Community Involvement**

Leaders and Sexual Assault Response Coordinators (SARCs) collaborate with community resources to extend and enhance the unit climate for personnel throughout the local community, both on and off-base to the extent authorized by law and Department of Defense regulations. This includes integrating prevention efforts with a variety of resources, including:

- Advocacy groups;
- Healthcare services providers;
- Family and social support service providers; and

- Researchers, university faculty, epidemiologists, and subject matter experts grounded in scientific data.

- **Deterrence**

A variety of tactics have been shown to help deter a wide range of negative behaviors. Commanders and their command teams, to include staff judge advocates, should collaborate with military and civilian law enforcement, Safety and Force Protection Officers, to determine the optimum mix of deterrence measures for their environment. Examples of potential tactics to deter criminal activity include:

- To the extent permissible by law and policy, publicizing court-martial results;
- Articulating lifetime costs of poor decisions;
- Surveillance measures (e.g., video cameras, patrols, barracks monitors); and
- Physical security enhancements.

- Communication

Messages promoting appropriate values, attitudes, and behaviors have shown great promise in achieving a healthy command climate and preventing sexual assaults. Commanders and command teams must visibly support and reinforce the messages. Messages must be appropriately tailored for the target audience(s). Commanders, SARCs, Public Affairs Officers, MCIOs, and Staff Judge Advocates should collaborate on how to message sexual assault prevention efforts and avoid unlawful command influence. Collaboration is encouraged with local experts and advocacy groups for ideas on what works in their community consistent with law and Department of Defense regulations. It is important to consider how to best use social media because of its prominence in delivering messages.

- **Incentives to Promote Prevention**

Recognition by leaders for establishing effective prevention programs or practices can incentivize units to be innovative and develop effective prevention programs and tactics. Examples of how incentives can be used include:

- Individuals recognized by leaders for safely intervening in incidents. Commanders must consider the risks and impacts when employing this tactic to determine the best means of delivery (e.g., public or private acknowledging);
- Volunteers awarded for conducting bystander intervention training; and
- Units awarded for effective, innovative prevention programs.

➢ **Harm Reduction (also called Risk Avoidance and Risk Reduction)**

Tactics that seek to reduce the risks of sexual assault show promise to help promote a healthy command climate. Commanders must review command climate surveys and discuss any threats to the welfare of the unit and individual members with their command team, SARC, and Safety Officer to identify potential tactics to reduce risks. These efforts can include a wide variety of risk mitigation (safety) programs and tactics that addresses both potential victims and perpetrators, including:

- Alcohol policies (e.g., alcohol storage in barracks, pricing, outlet density);
- Collaboration with management of establishments Service members are likely to visit on and off base;
- Courses that instruct and empower members through awareness, violence intervention, and self-defense techniques;
- Unit sponsorship for new members; and
- Ongoing command monitoring of individuals who are demonstrating problem behaviors (e.g., documented history of sexual violence, sexual harassment, alcohol or drug abuse, hazing).

➢ **Education and Training**

Education and training efforts designed to improve knowledge, impart a skill, and/or influence attitudes and behaviors of a target population are an important part of a prevention program. Courses should teach bystander intervention, victim empathy, consent, acceptable behavior, and healthy relationships. The curriculum should be evidence-based, adapted to the environment, and responsive to the gender, culture, beliefs, and diverse needs of the targeted audiences. Education and training must be properly designed following adult learning principles and be delivered by well-trained professionals, or it risks being ineffective or having a negative impact. The following training practices were included in promising sexual assault prevention education and training programs:

- Multiple lessons/sessions to reinforce key messages and provide opportunities to practice new skills;
- Peer educators to deliver training program;
- Interactive format (minimize lecture, focus on discussion, role-play, and exercises);
- Real life scenarios (discuss scenarios and the appropriate responses); and
- Culture-specific content and messages (allow each installation, and potentially each command, to customize the training content to their specific culture and participant levels).

6. Prevention Metrics, Assessment, and Research

6.1. Prevention Key Metrics

DoD has identified several key intermediary and long term measures of effectiveness to assess prevention efforts (see ***Figure 6***). DoD uses these metrics as a standard set of measures to evaluate prevention efforts across all the Services. These metrics are not all inclusive. The Services are encouraged to continually assess their programs using additional metrics (e.g., surveys, focus groups, or physical observations).

6.2. Prevention Assessment and Research

DoD will conduct assessments and research, such as those listed below, in an effort to better understand the effectiveness of our prevention efforts.

Expand Military Research to Inform Future Prevention Efforts

A critical component of our prevention effort is based on a detailed understanding of those who commit sexual harassment and sexual assault or contribute to the establishment of an environment that allows it. DoD will study interventions at all levels of the SEM to determine their effectiveness.

#	Metric Name	Metric Definition	Rationale for Measurement	Projected Data Sources
1	Past Year Prevalence of Unwanted Sexual Contact	Measures Service Member experience with unwanted sexual contact in the year prior to being surveyed.	Provides best estimate of sexual assault incidents involving Service member victims ("Extent of the Problem")	WGRA & WGRR
2	Prevalence vs. Reporting	Measures the percentage of Service member incidents captured in reports of sexual assault (Restricted +Unrestricted Reports)	Provides estimate of the proportion of the crime being reported	WGRA + DSAID
3	Bystander Intervention Experience in Past 12 months	Service member responses to: "In the past 12 months, I observed a situation that I believed to be at risk for sexual assault" and how they intervened	–Indicator of Service member actions to prevent sexual assault	DEOCS
4	Command Climate Index – Addressing Continuum of Harm	Service Member Index of Responses to: - Promote a unit climate based on "mutual respect and trust" - Refrain from sexist comments and behaviors - Actively discourage sexist comments and behaviors	–Indicators of a healthy command climate –Indicator of prevention that addresses continuum of harm	DEOCS

Legend:
DEOCS = DEOMI Equal Opportunity Climate Survey
DSAID = Defense Sexual Assault Incident Database
WGRA = Workplace and Gender Relations Survey of Active Duty Members
WGRR = Workplace and Gender Relations Survey of Reserve Component Members

Figure 6.

Reinforcing Early Prevention Efforts

Recognizing the importance of early prevention interventions, DoD will review current middle and high school programs, to include the DODEA schools and Junior Reserve Officer Training Corps programs for promising practices to identify programs which promote healthy relationships and active bystander intervention using evidence-based methods.

Conduct Research to Better Understand Male Victimology

Recognizing that anonymous surveys indicate that many victims are male, DoD will conduct research to understand the situations that give rise to male victimization and the special needs that male survivors may have. This research will be used to develop effective strategies, policies, and messaging to improve targeted prevention interventions for men.

Evaluate Prevention Focus on Continuum of Harm

Recognizing the connection between preventing sexual assault in terms of the continuum of harm (e.g., sexist jokes, bullying, sexual harassment, hazing, drinking, stalking), DoD will evaluate the feasibility of creating a new credentialed position focused on programs needed to advance prevention behavior across that spectrum. DoD will determine the feasibility of those handling sexual harassment and Sexual Assault Response Coordinators/Victim Advocates focusing solely on victim care, and having this new position manage prevention efforts that would incorporate both sexual harassment and sexual assault.

APPENDIX A: DEPARTMENT OF DEFENSE SEXUAL ASSAULT PREVENTION AND RESPONSE STRATEGIC PLAN PREVENTION TASKS FOR REVISED STRATEGY

As a result of the collaboration and collective efforts of the DoD SAPR community, offered below is a list of the targeted tasks identified to realize the Prevention LOE end state in the *DoD SAPR Strategic Plan*. The following section captures the tasks defined by plan owners to be pursued and executed. Specific details about plan progress and milestones shall be provided by the respective participating organizations. ***Figure*** *7* contains a key to explain the information contained in each of the task columns.

Since this plan captures planning components from different organizations, each organization designated in the task matrix as office of primary responsibility (OPR) is responsible for accomplishing its designated tasks and supporting actions and /or initiatives. For this reason, plan components may be written at different levels and stress different activities. However, the collective stakeholders are committed to the same strategic objectives and end states.

Accomplishment of the prevention tasks ***Figure 8*** will help to achieve the *2013 DoD SAPR Strategic Plan* Prevention LOE objective to deliver consistent and effective prevention methods and overarching prevention end state to ensure cultural imperatives of mutual respect and trust, professional values, and team commitment are reinforced to create an environment where sexual assault is not tolerated, condoned, or ignored.

Task Key:
Time: Short = 0 to 1 Year (from date of publication) Med = 1 to 2 Years Long = 2 to 3 Years Continual = On-going/Cyclic Requirement
Priority = Importance to overall strategy; 1 being the most important
OPR = Office of Primary Responsibility
** = Action outlined in *Strategic Direction to the Joint Force on SAPR*
++ = Provision published in NDAA FY12
^^ = Provision published in NDAA FY13
= Provision published in NDAA FY14

Figure 7.

Prevention Tasks	**Time**	**Pri.**	**OPRs**
Implement the 2014-2016 DoD Sexual Assault Prevention Strategy.	Short	1	All
Conduct specialized leader sexual assault prevention training.	Short	2	Military Departments & Services, NGB

Prevention Tasks	Time	Pri.	OPRs
Develop and expand gender-responsive and culturally competent programs (e.g., mentorship, initial entry) to address healthy relationships and active bystander intervention —with the emphasis that core values should anchor all actions— in order to support the establishment of a culture of mutual respect.	Short	3	Military Departments & Services, NGB
Review and if necessary expand DoD and Service alcohol policies to address factors beyond individual use (e.g., pricing, outlet density, *Arizona Safer Bars Alliance*).	Short	4	Military Departments & Services, NGB
Develop a process for command review of information on sex-related offenses in personnel service records of members of the Armed Forces (for purpose of reducing likelihood that repeat offenses will escape notice) in accordance with section 1745 of the National Defense Authorization Act for Fiscal Year 2014.##	Short	5	Military Departments & Services, NGB
Explore the development of (enhancement of existing) sexual assault deterrence measures and messaging (e.g., publishing court-martial results).	Med	6	Military Departments & Services, NGB, SAPRO
Assess, implement core competencies, and continue to update all sexual assault prevention-related training and programs based on latest evidenced based research, practices, and lessons- learned.**++^^ ##	Continual	7	Military Departments & Services, SAPRO
Implement policies that appropriately address high-risk situations targeted by offenders.**	Long	8	Military Departments & Services, NGB
Institute recurring senior leadership meetings (e.g., quarterly FO/GO drumbeat, leader summits) to review sexual assault prevention programs (not case management group meeting).	Med	9	Military Departments & Services, NGB
Identify and implement incentives for the prevention of sexual assault and other related behaviors (e.g., alcohol abuse, sexual harassment, hazing).	Long	10	Military Departments & Services, NGB, SAPRO

Figure 8. (Continued).

Develop a military community of practice focused on primary prevention of sexual assault.	Short	11	SAPRO
Establish collaboration forums with external experts, federal partners, Military Services, advocacy organizations, and educational institutions to capture and share prevention best practices and lessons learned in accordance with Federal law and Department regulations.	Continual	12	Military Departments & Services, SAPRO
Develop a prevention guide that outlines promising practices and lessons learned in sexual assault prevention.	Short	13	SAPRO
Review national (e.g., state, university), and coalition (e.g., U.K. and Canada) sexual assault prevention programs to identify best practices and lessons learned.	Continual	14	SAPRO
Develop sexual assault prevention strategies and programs which employ peers, near-peers (i.e., Service member one rank higher or somewhat senior in position of authority), and social influencers.	Continual	15	Military Departments & Services, NGB
Incorporate specific sexual assault monitoring, measures, and education into normal command training, readiness assessments, and safety forums (e.g., SAPR stand downs).**	Continual	16	Military Departments & Services, NGB
Assess transition policies that ensure Service member sponsorship, unit integration, and immediate assignment into a chain of command.**	Continual	17	Military Departments & Services, NGB
Identify and implement sexual assault prevention tools (e.g., mobile apps, leader toolkits).	Med	18	SAPRO

Figure 8.

APPENDIX B: DEFINING THE THREAT AND ENVIRONMENT

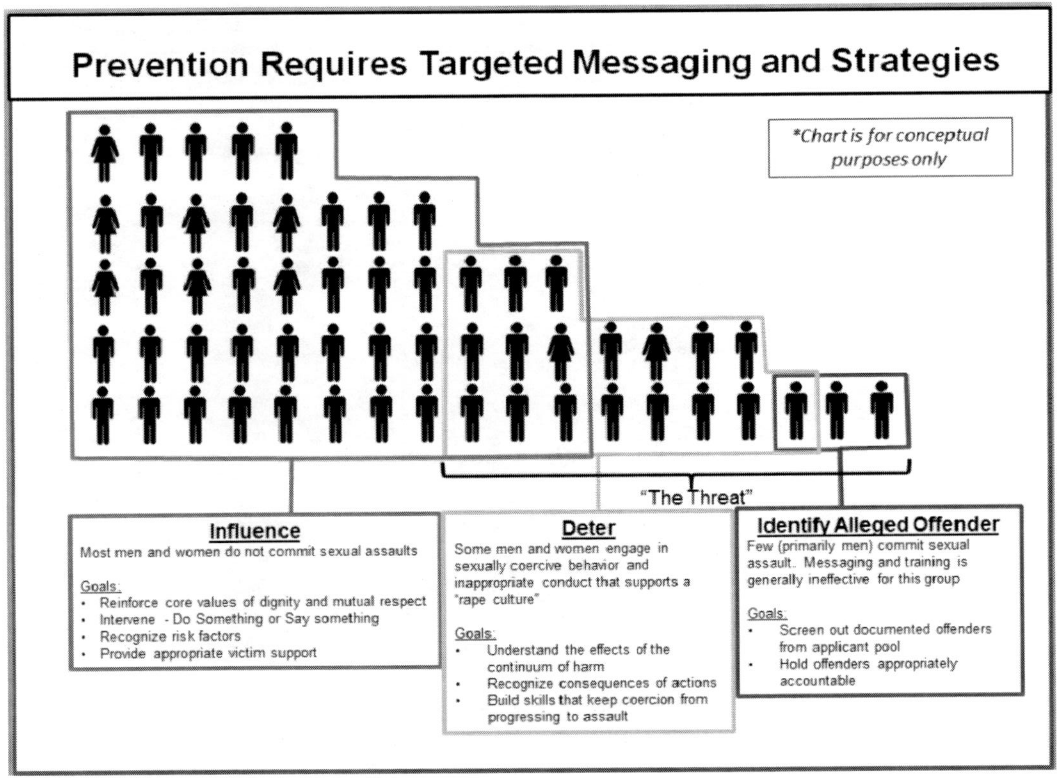

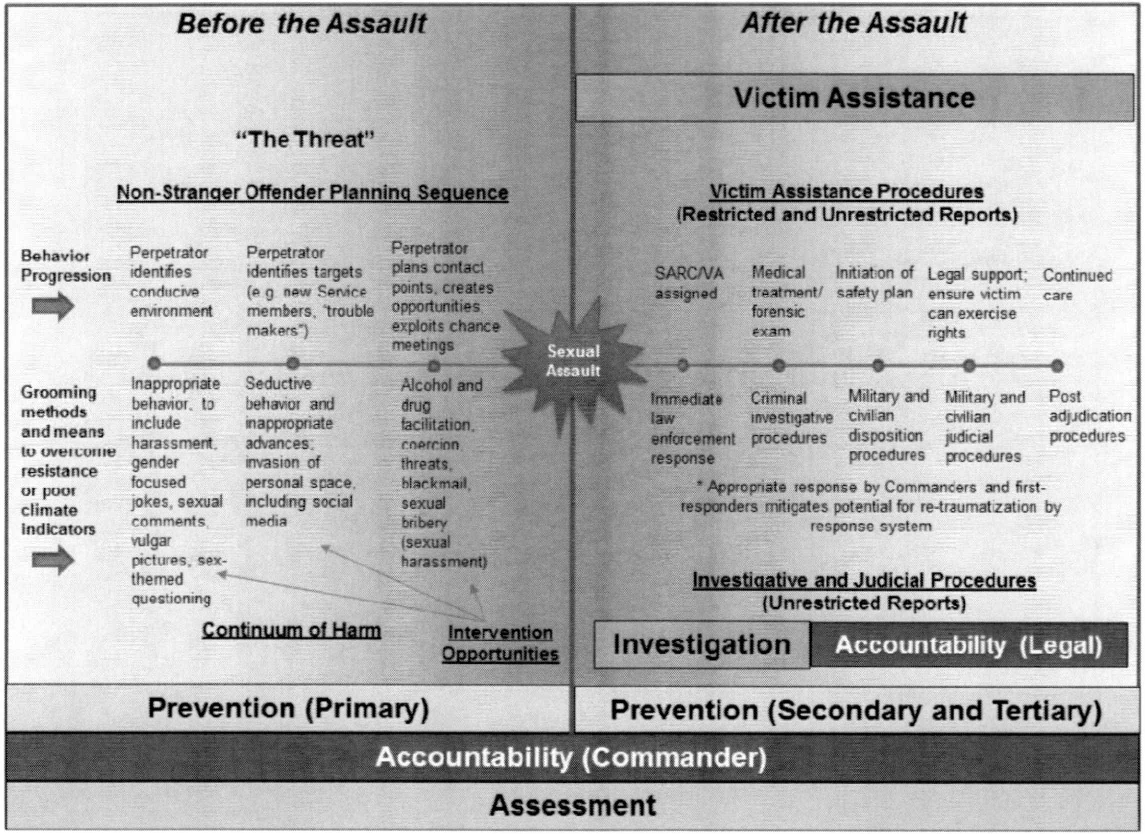

Before the Assault
After the Assault
Victim Assistance
"The Threat"
Non-Stranger Offender Planning Sequence
Behavior Progression
Perpetrator identifies conducive environment
Perpetrator identifies targets (e.g. new Service members, "trouble makers")
Perpetrator plans contact points, creates opportunities exploits chance meetings
Sexual Assault
Grooming methods and means to overcome resistance or poor climate indicators
Inappropriate behavior, to include harassment, gender focused jokes, sexual comments, vulgar pictures, sex-themed questioning
Seductive behavior and inappropriate advances; invasion of personal space, including social media
Alcohol and drug facilitation, coercion threats, blackmail, sexual bribery (sexual harassment)
Continuum of Harm
Intervention Opportunities
Victim Assistance Procedures
(Restricted and Unrestricted Reports)
SARC/VA assigned
Medical treatment/ forensic exam
Initiation of safety plan
Legal support; ensure victim can exercise rights
Continued care
Immediate law enforcement response
Criminal investigative procedures
Military and civilian disposition procedures
Military and civilian judicial procedures
Post adjudication procedures
* Appropriate response by Commanders and first-responders mitigates potential for re-traumatization by response system
Investigative and Judicial Procedures
(Unrestricted Reports)
Investigation
Accountability (Legal)
Prevention (Primary)
Prevention (Secondary and Tertiary)
Accountability (Commander)
Assessment

Appendix C: Sexual Violence Risk and Protective Factors (as identified by CDC)

Individual Risk Factors

- Alcohol and drug use
- Coercive sexual fantasies
- Impulsive and antisocial tendencies
- Preference for impersonal sex
- Hostility towards women
- Hypermasculinity
- Childhood history of sexual and physical abuse
- Witnessed family violence as a child

Relationship Risk Factors

- Association with sexually aggressive and delinquent peers
- Family environment characterized by physical violence and few resources
- Strong patriarchal relationship or familial environment
- Emotionally unsupportive familial environment

Community Risk Factors

- Lack of employment opportunities
- Lack of institutional support from police and judicial system
- General tolerance of sexual violence within the community
- Weak community sanctions against sexual violence perpetrators

Societal Risk Factors

- Poverty
- Societal norms that support sexual violence
- Societal norms that support male superiority and sexual entitlement

- Societal norms that maintain women's inferiority and sexual submissiveness
- Weak laws and policies related to gender equity
- High tolerance levels of crime and other forms of violence[1]

Protective Factors

- Emotional health and connectedness (high school boys)
- Academic achievement (high school girls)
- "Loss of face,"—a concern for how one's actions affect others (among Asian American men)
- Parents use of reasoning to resolve family conflicts (males)
- Effect varied by risk factor; for example, loss of face, but not hostile masculinity, protected against the effect of early risk factors on sexual violence
- Empathy had several direct and indirect effects

APPENDIX D: REFERENCES

Reference
2008 Department of Defense Sexual Assault Prevention Strategy
Strategic Direction to the Joint Force on Sexual Assault Prevention and Response, May 2012
2013 Department of Defense Sexual Assault Prevention and Response Strategic Plan
Workplace and Gender Relations Survey of Active Duty Members (WGRA), Defense Manpower Data Center (DMDC), 15 March 2013
Department of Defense Annual Report on Sexual Assault in the Military, Fiscal Year 2012, 9 May 2013
Department of Defense Instruction (Sexual Assault Prevention and Response (SAPR) Program Procedures) 6495.02, 28 March 2013

Appendix E: Definitions

Arizona Safer Bars Alliance. A statewide comprehensive bystander intervention training program designed for alcohol-serving establishments. Bar managers, bouncers, and servers are trained to identify and stop predatory or sexually aggressive behaviors associated with sexual assault. This program is currently used in Arizona and 16 other states.

Bystander intervention. *The willingness to safely take action and help someone in time of need.*

Center of Gravity. The source of power that provides moral or physical strength, freedom of action, or will to act.

Continuum of Harm. In the context of sexual violence, the continuum of harm refers to inappropriate actions, such as sexist jokes, hazing, cyber bullying, that are used before or after the assault and or supports an environment which tolerates these actions.

Consent. A freely given agreement to the conduct at issue by a competent person. An expression of lack of consent through words or conduct means there is no consent. Lack of verbal or physical resistance or submission resulting from the use of force, threat of force, or placing another person in fear does not constitute consent. A current or previous dating or social or sexual relationship by itself or the manner of dress of the person involved with the accused in the conduct at issue shall not constitute consent. A sleeping, unconscious, or incompetent person cannot consent.

Healthy relationships. A healthy functional intimate relationship that is based on equality and respect, not power and control.

Intervention. A deliberate process by which change is introduced into peoples' thoughts, feelings and behaviors.

Sexual assault. Intentional sexual contact characterized by the use of force, threats, intimidation, or abuse of authority or when the victim does not or cannot consent. As used in this strategy, the term includes a broad category of sexual offenses consisting of the following specific UCMJ offenses: rape, sexual assault, aggravated sexual contact, abusive sexual contact, forcible sodomy (forced oral or anal sex), or attempts to commit these offenses.

Sexual violence. CDC defines sexual violence (SV) as any sexual act that is perpetrated against someone's will. SV encompasses a range of offenses, including a completed nonconsensual sex act (i.e., rape), an attempted nonconsensual sex act, abusive sexual contact (i.e., unwanted touching), and non-contact sexual abuse (e.g., threatened sexual violence, exhibitionism, verbal sexual harassment). These four types are defined in more detail below.

All types involve victims who do not consent, or who are unable to consent or refuse to allow the act.

- **A completed sex act** is defined as contact between the penis and the vulva or the penis and the anus involving penetration, however slight; contact between the mouth and penis, vulva, or anus; or penetration of the anal or genital opening of another person by a hand, finger, or other object.
- **An attempted (but not completed) sex act**
- **Abusive sexual contact** is defined as intentional touching, either directly or through the clothing, of the genitalia, anus, groin, breast, inner thigh, or buttocks of any person without his or her consent, or of a person who is unable to consent or refuse.
- **Non-contact sexual abuse** does not include physical contact of a sexual nature between the perpetrator and the victim. It includes acts such as voyeurism; intentional exposure of an individual to exhibitionism; unwanted exposure to pornography; verbal or behavioral sexual harassment; threats of sexual violence to accomplish some other end; or taking nude photographs of a sexual nature of another person without his or her consent or knowledge, or of a person who is unable to consent or refuse.

Social influencers. Influential members of a community, group, or society to whom others turn for advice, opinions, and views.

Unwanted sexual contact. The survey term for the contact sex crimes between adults that constitute sexual assault under military law. These crimes range from non-penetrating crimes such as groping, to penetrating crimes such as rape.

Victim empathy. The cognitive and emotional understanding of the experience of the victim.

End Notes

[1] The Joint Chiefs of Staff, Strategic Direction to the Joint Force on Sexual Assault Prevention and Response, 7 May 2012

[2] Sexual violence prevention: beginning the dialogue. Atlanta, GA: Centers for Disease Control and Prevention; 2004.

[3] This widely adapted prevention concept was articulated by Gordon in 1987 and promoted by the Institute of Medicine in 1994.

[4] Workplace and Gender Relations Surveys of Active Duty Members. Defense Manpower Data Center. Years 2006, 2010 and 2012. Given many respondents experienced more than one incident of unwanted sexual contact, the survey asked respondents to consider the one situation that had the greatest effect on them and asked details about that incident. Reserve Component data is collected in a separate survey.

[5] Unwanted sexual contact is the survey term for the contact sex crimes between adults that constitute sexual assault under military law. These crimes range from non-penetrating crimes such as groping, to penetrating crimes such as rape.

[6] Attitudinal, experiential, and situational predictors of sexual assault perpetration, Journal of Interpersonal Violence, Abbey A, McAusland P, Zawacki T, Clinton AM, Buck PO. 2001:784–807. Perception of sexual intent: The role of gender, alcohol consumption, and rape supportive attitudes, Abbey A, Harnish RJ. Sex Roles 1995.

[7] Factors Associated with Women's Risk of Rape in the Military Environment, American Journal of Industrial Medicine, Anne G. Sadler; 2003

[8] Sexual Assault and Other Types of Sexual Harassment by Workplace Peronnel: A Comparison of Antecedents and Consequences, Journal of Occupational Health Psychology, Melanie Harned, Alayne Ormerod Patrick Palmieri, Linda Collinsworth, and Magie Reed; 2002.

[9] Sexual violence prevention: beginning the dialogue. Atlanta, GA: Centers for Disease Control and Prevention; 2004.

[10] The DoD defines promising practice as an identified practice that shows demonstrable beneficial impact, for at least one organization, and shows promise during its early stages for becoming a best practice with long term sustainable impact; some basis for claiming effectiveness.

End Note for Appendix C

[1] Briefing given to DoD SAPRO by U.S. Centers for Disease Control and Prevention, November 2013 and CDC website, http://www.cdc.gov/violenceprevention/sexualviolence/risk protectivefactors.html.

In: Sexual Assault Prevention ...
Editor: Jonathan Maldonado ISBN: 978-1-63485-351-4

Chapter 2

SEXUAL ASSAULT: ACTIONS NEEDED TO IMPROVE DOD'S PREVENTION STRATEGY AND TO HELP ENSURE IT IS EFFECTIVELY IMPLEMENTED*

United States Government Accountability Office

WHY GAO DID THIS STUDY

Sexual assault is a crime that devastates victims and has a far-reaching negative impact for DOD because it undermines DOD's core values, degrades mission readiness, and raises financial costs. DOD data show that reported sexual assaults involving servicemembers more than doubled from about 2,800 reports in fiscal year 2007 to about 6,100 reports in fiscal year 2014. Based on results of a 2014 survey, RAND estimated that 20,300 active-duty servicemembers were sexually assaulted in the prior year.

Senate Report 113-176 includes a provision for GAO to review DOD's efforts to prevent sexual assault. This report addresses the extent to which DOD (1) developed an effective prevention strategy, (2) implemented activities department-wide and at military installations related to the department's effort to prevent sexual assault, and (3) developed performance measures to determine the effectiveness of its efforts to prevent sexual assault

* This is an edited, reformatted and augmented version of a United States Government Accountability Office, Publication No. GAO-16-61, dated November 2015.

in the military. GAO evaluated DOD's strategy against CDC's framework for effective sexual-violence prevention strategies, reviewed DOD policies, and interviewed cognizant officials.

WHAT GAO RECOMMENDS

GAO recommends that DOD link prevention activities with desired outcomes; identify risk and protective factors for all domains; communicate and disseminate its strategy to all program personnel; align service policies with the strategy; and fully develop performance measures. DOD concurred with all recommendations and noted actions it was taking.

WHAT GAO FOUND

The Department of Defense (DOD) developed its strategy to prevent sexual assault using the Centers for Disease Control and Prevention (CDC) framework for effective sexual-violence prevention strategies, but DOD does not link activities to desired outcomes or fully identify risk and protective factors. Specifically, DOD's strategy identifies 18 prevention-related activities, but they are not linked to desired outcomes—a step that CDC says is necessary to determine whether efforts are producing the intended effect. CDC has also demonstrated that by identifying risk and protective factors—relative to the domain or environment in which they exist—organizations can focus efforts on eliminating risk factors that promote sexual violence while also supporting the protective factors that prevent it. DOD identifies five domains in its strategy and includes risk factors for three—individuals, relationships, and society—but it does not specify risk factors for the other two domains—leaders at all levels of DOD and the military community. Further, DOD does not specify how the protective factors, such as emotional health, identified in its strategy relate to the five domains. Thus, DOD may be limited in its ability to take an evidence-based approach to the prevention of sexual assault.

DOD and the military services are in the process of implementing prevention-focused activities, but they have not taken steps to ensure that installation-level activities are consistent with the overarching objectives of DOD's strategy. DOD's strategy identifies 18 activities, 2 of which DOD considers implemented while efforts to address the remaining 16 are ongoing.

For example, DOD officials report that they have implemented the activity directing the development of a military community of practice. Additionally, GAO identified activities that had been developed and implemented at the four installations GAO visited, but found that they may not be consistent with DOD's strategy because it has not been communicated or disseminated to the personnel responsible for implementing the activities. Further, service policies—key conduits of such communication—do not provide the guidance necessary to unify the department's prevention efforts because they have not been updated to align with and operationalize the principles outlined in DOD's most recent strategy. Thus, DOD cannot be sure that all prevention-related activities are achieving the goals and objectives of the department's strategy.

DOD has identified five performance measures to assess the effectiveness of its prevention efforts, but these measures are not fully developed as they are missing many of the 10 key attributes that GAO has found can contribute to assessing program performance effectively, such as baseline and trend data, measurable target, and clarity. Specifically, all five performance measures demonstrate some of these attributes but collectively they are missing more than half of these attributes. All of the prevention efforts' measures demonstrate baseline and trend data but none of the measures have measurable target, clarity, and some of the other attributes. Without fully developed measures, DOD and other decision makers may not be able to effectively gauge the progress of the department's prevention efforts.

ABBREVIATIONS

CDC	Centers for Disease Control and Prevention
DEOCS	Defense Equal Opportunity Management Institute Organizational Climate Survey
DEOMI	Defense Equal Opportunity Management Institute
DOD	Department of Defense
NDAA	National Defense Authorization Act
OSD	Office of the Secretary of Defense
SAPR	Sexual Assault Prevention and Response
SAPRO	Sexual Assault Prevention and Response Office
SARC	Sexual Assault Response Coordinator
SECNAVINST	Secretary of the Navy Instructions
WGRA	Workplace and Gender Relations Survey of Active Duty Members

November 4, 2015

The Honorable John McCain
Chairman
The Honorable Jack Reed
Ranking Member
Committee on Armed Services
United States Senate

The Honorable Mac Thornberry
Chairman
The Honorable Adam Smith
Ranking Member
Committee on Armed Services
House of Representatives

Sexual assault is a crime that devastates victims and has a far-reaching negative effect for the Department of Defense (DOD) because it undermines the department's core values, degrades mission readiness and esprit de corps, subverts strategic goodwill, and raises financial costs. DOD data show that the number of reported sexual assaults involving military servicemembers more than doubled from about 2,800 reports in fiscal year 2007 to about 6,100 reports in fiscal year 2014.[1] However, recent data suggest that these reports represent a fraction of the sexual assault incidents that are actually occurring. Specifically, based on the results of its 2014 Military Workplace Study, the RAND Corporation estimated that about 20,300 active-duty servicemembers were sexually assaulted in the year prior to the survey.[2] While the increase in reports since fiscal year 2007 and the most recent estimated number of servicemember victims are significant, sexual assault is an underreported crime, and DOD officials believe the increase in reporting reflects the growing confidence of servicemembers in the department's response to victims as opposed to a decrease in the effectiveness of its prevention efforts. According to DOD, sexual assault continues to represent a significant and persistent problem within the department and DOD has considerable interest in better preventing it.

For over a decade, Congress and DOD have taken a variety of steps to prevent sexual assault in the military. In 2004, following a series of high-profile sexual assault cases involving servicemembers, Congress required the Secretary of Defense to develop, among other things, a comprehensive policy for DOD on the prevention of sexual assaults involving servicemembers.[3] In response to statutory requirements, DOD established its sexual-assault prevention and response program in 2005, and has taken a variety of other steps aimed at improving the department's efforts to prevent sexual assault. For example, in 2008, DOD published its first sexual-assault prevention strategy. In April 2014, DOD updated its strategy (calling it the 2014–16 sexual-assault prevention strategy). For additional information on efforts identified by DOD in its 2014 Report to the President of the United States on Sexual Assault Prevention and Response that it took to improve the prevention of sexual assault in the military since 2013, see appendix I.

Since 2008, we have issued multiple products and made numerous recommendations related to DOD's efforts to prevent and respond to incidents of sexual assault. Most recently, in March 2015, we reported on the extent to which DOD has taken actions to prevent and respond to sexual assaults of male servicemembers.[4] We found that DOD had not used all of its data to inform program decision making, had not established goals or metrics to gauge sexual assault–related issues for male servicemembers, and had generally not portrayed male sexual-assault victims in its sexual-assault prevention training material. Based on our findings, we recommended that DOD, among other things, develop a plan for using its data to inform program development, develop associated goals and metrics, and revise training to address male victims. DOD concurred with all six of the recommendations in our 2015 report and is in the process of implementing them. For additional information on our prior work related to sexual assault in the military, see appendix II as well as the Related GAO Products page at the end of this report.

In June 2014, the Senate Armed Services Committee report accompanying a bill for the National Defense Authorization Act for Fiscal Year 2015 included a provision that we report on various efforts by DOD to prevent sexual assault in the military.[5] This report addresses the extent to which DOD has (1) developed an effective prevention strategy,[6] (2) implemented activities department-wide and at service-specific and joint installations related to the department's effort to prevent sexual assault in the military,[7] and (3) developed performance measures to determine the effectiveness of its efforts to prevent sexual assault in the military.

For our first objective, we reviewed DOD's 2014-16 Sexual Assault Prevention Strategy and other relevant guidance and requirements from DOD and the military services on the prevention of sexual assault and interviewed officials in DOD's Sexual Assault Prevention and Response Office (SAPRO) and from each military service on their efforts to implement this guidance and prevent sexual assault. We also interviewed officials from the Centers for Disease Control and Prevention (CDC) who are the federal government's focal point for sexual-violence prevention and have experience working with sexual-violence prevention programs. We used CDC's social-ecological model and public-health model to assess DOD's 2014-16 Sexual Assault Prevention Strategy and associated documents.[8] Specifically, we used these models to assess the extent to which DOD's 2014–16 prevention strategy and related documents contain elements that CDC has identified as providing a framework for developing and implementing effective sexual-violence prevention programs. We used Office of Management and Budget guidance on conducting agency strategic reviews and mitigating risks related to achieving strategic objectives and performance goals. We also used our prior work on effective agency strategic reviews, which has shown that it is important to review progress toward strategic objectives in that it can help to determine subsequent actions and that leaders and responsible managers should be held accountable for knowing the progress being made in achieving outcomes.[9]

For our second objective, we reviewed DOD and military service sexual-assault prevention and response policies and guidance, which included DOD's 2014-16 Sexual Assault Prevention Strategy, to identify activities related to the prevention of sexual assault. We also interviewed various officials with responsibilities related to the prevention of sexual assault at four military installations in the United States—two for the Army, one for the Marine Corps, and one joint base that included the Navy and the Air Force—to obtain their perspectives on DOD's efforts to prevent sexual assault.[10] During our visits to these installations, we met with commanders, sexual-assault response coordinators (SARC), sexual harassment/assault response and prevention program managers, victim advocates, chaplains, criminal investigators, legal personnel, and medical- and mental-healthcare providers to obtain their perspectives on DOD-wide prevention efforts as well as those being developed and implemented within their respective service.

For our third objective, we reviewed relevant program guidance and related documents and met with DOD and military-service officials to discuss the performance measures that DOD developed to assess its overall efforts to prevent sexual assault in the military. In addition, we compared DOD's prevention-focused performance measures with GAO criteria on key attributes of successful performance measures.[11] Additionally, we met with DOD and military-service officials to discuss the performance measures identified and how DOD plans to use them to assess the effectiveness of their strategy for and efforts to prevent sexual assault.

We conducted this performance audit from August 2014 to October 2015 in accordance with generally accepted government auditing standards. Those standards require that we plan and perform the audit to obtain sufficient, appropriate evidence to provide a reasonable basis for our findings and conclusions based on our audit objectives. We believe that the evidence obtained provides a reasonable basis for our findings and conclusions based on our audit objectives. Further details of our scope and methodology are presented in appendix III.

BACKGROUND

Definition of Sexual Assault

DOD defines sexual assault as intentional sexual contact, characterized by use of force, threats, intimidation, abuse of authority, or when the victim does not or cannot consent. The term includes a broad category of sexual offenses consisting of the following specific Uniform Code of Military Justice offenses: rape, sexual assault, aggravated sexual contact, abusive sexual contact, forcible sodomy (forced oral or anal sex), or attempts to commit these acts.[12]

Centers for Disease Control and Prevention (CDC) and Its Sexual Violence Prevention Efforts

CDC is one of the major operating components of the Department of Health and Human Services, which serves as the federal government's principal agency for protecting the health of all U.S. citizens. As part of its health-related mission, CDC serves as the national focal point for developing and applying disease prevention and control, environmental health, and health promotion and education activities. Specifically, CDC, among other things, conducts research to enhance prevention, develops and advocates public-health policies, implements prevention strategies, promotes healthy behaviors, fosters safe and healthful environments, and provides associated training.

In 1992, CDC established the National Center for Injury Prevention and Control as the lead federal organization for violence prevention. The center's Division of Violence Prevention focuses on stopping violence, including sexual violence, before it begins, and it works to achieve this by conducting research on the factors that put people at risk for violence, examining the effective adoption and dissemination of prevention strategies, and evaluating the effectiveness of violence-prevention programs. In addition, CDC operates the Rape Prevention and Education grant program in all 50 states, the District of Columbia, Puerto Rico, and four U.S. territories to strengthen sexual-violence prevention efforts at the local, state, and national level.

In 2004, CDC published a framework for effective sexual-violence prevention strategies. This framework includes prevention concepts and strategies, such as identifying risk and protective factors (i.e., factors that may put a person at risk for committing sexual assault or that, alternatively, may prevent harm). CDC suggests that grantees of the Rape Prevention and Education program use this framework as a foundation for planning, implementing, and evaluating activities conducted.

DOD's Sexual Assault Prevention and Response Program

Since fiscal year 2004, Congress has mandated, and in response DOD has implemented, a number of improvements to its sexual-assault prevention and response program. For example, in 2004, Congress required the Secretary of Defense to develop a comprehensive policy for DOD on the prevention of and response to sexual assaults involving servicemembers and to submit an annual report that includes, among other things, data on reported incidents within each military service and the results of an evaluation of the effectiveness of DOD's sexual-assault prevention and response policy.[13] In 2005, DOD established its sexual-assault prevention and response program to promote the prevention of sexual assault, to encourage increased reporting of such incidents, and to improve victim response capabilities; and DOD has issued annual reports tracking the number of sexual assaults reported each year.

Since that time, DOD has undertaken a variety of activities both to prevent sexual assaults from occurring and to increase the department's visibility over and awareness of sexual-assault incidents that do occur. Specifically, in response to statutory requirements, DOD has provided active-duty servicemembers with two options for reporting a sexual assault: (1) restricted and (2) unrestricted. DOD's restricted reporting option allows sexual-assault victims to confidentially disclose an alleged sexual assault to select individuals and receive medical and mental health-care treatment without initiating an official investigation. In cases where a victim elects restricted reporting, first responders may not disclose confidential communications to law-enforcement or command authorities unless certain exceptions apply, and improper disclosure of confidential communications and medical information may result in discipline pursuant to the Uniform Code of Military Justice or other adverse personnel actions. In contrast, DOD's unrestricted reporting option triggers an investigation by a military criminal-investigative organization. In an effort to increase victims' confidence in the military-justice process and to encourage reporting, DOD revised its sexual-assault prevention and response policy in January 2012 to protect victims of sexual assault from coercion, retaliation, and reprisal.[14]

DOD Entities with Key Roles and Responsibilities in the Prevention of Sexual Assault

Various offices and organizations within DOD play a role in preventing and responding to sexual assault within the military. The Under Secretary of Defense for Personnel and Readiness is responsible for developing the overall policy and guidance for the department's sexual-assault prevention and response program, except for criminal-investigative policy matters assigned to the DOD Inspector General and legal processes in the Uniform Code of Military Justice. Accordingly, the Under Secretary of Defense for Personnel and Readiness oversees SAPRO, which serves as the department's single point of authority, accountability, and oversight for its sexual-assault prevention and response program. The responsibilities of the Under Secretary of Defense for Personnel and Readiness and SAPRO with regard to sexual-assault prevention and response include providing the military services with guidance and technical support and facilitating the identification and resolution of issues; developing programs, policies, and training standards for the prevention of, reporting of, and response to sexual assault; developing strategic program guidance and joint planning objectives; overseeing the department's collection and maintenance of data on reported alleged sexual assaults involving servicemembers; establishing mechanisms to measure the effectiveness of the department's sexual-assault prevention and response program; and preparing the department's mandated annual reports to Congress on sexual assaults involving servicemembers.[15]

Each military service has established a sexual-assault prevention and response office that is responsible for overseeing and managing the service's sexual-assault program.[16] Each military service has also established the SARC position to serve as the single point of contact for ensuring that sexual-assault victims receive appropriate and responsive care and are generally responsible for implementing their respective services' SAPR program. According to DOD's instruction, commanders, supervisors, and managers at all levels are responsible for the effective implementation of both the policy and the program.[17] Other responders include victim advocates, judge advocates, medical and mental healthcare providers, criminal-investigative personnel, law-enforcement personnel, and chaplains.

The Secretaries of the military departments are responsible for establishing policies to implement the sexual-assault prevention and response program and procedures, and ensuring compliance with DOD's policy. Further, they are responsible for establishing policies that ensure commander accountability for program implementation and execution. Each military service maintains a primary policy document on its sexual-assault prevention and response program.[18] Much like DOD's directive and instruction on sexual-assault prevention and response, the service policies outline responsibilities of relevant stakeholders, including commanders, SARCs, and victim advocates, and training requirements for all personnel.

DOD Used CDC Guidance to Develop Its Sexual-Assault Prevention Strategy but It Did Not Specify How Related Activities Are Linked to Desired Outcomes or Fully Identify Factors Needed to Focus Its Prevention Efforts

DOD developed its sexual-assault prevention strategy in 2014 using CDC's framework for effective sexual-violence prevention strategies, but DOD did not link prevention activities to desired outcomes or fully identify risk and protective factors. Specifically, DOD identified 18 prevention-related activities in its strategy, but did not specify how these activities are linked with the desired outcomes of the department's overall prevention efforts. Further, in adapting CDC's framework to address the unique nature of the military environment, DOD did not fully identify risk and protective factors (i.e., factors that may put a person at risk for committing sexual assault or that, alternatively, may prevent harm) in its updated strategy.

DOD Updated Its Sexual-Assault Prevention Strategy to Include Some Concepts That CDC Developed for Effective Sexual-Violence Prevention Strategies

In April 2014, DOD published an updated prevention strategy using concepts from CDC's framework for effective sexual-violence prevention strategies. Following guidance outlined by the Secretary of Defense in the 2013 Department of Defense Sexual Assault Prevention and Response Strategic Plan, SAPRO developed and executed a sexual-assault prevention campaign to identify evidence-based prevention practices and lessons learned, in order to update the department's 2008 Sexual Assault Prevention Strategy.[19] Though not required to do so, DOD consulted with and incorporated CDC's framework and prevention-related concepts into its prevention strategy. Specifically, DOD incorporated CDC's concept that defines the different levels at which prevention efforts occur and another CDC concept that describes the importance of identifying and understanding the domains in which sexual violence takes place. For example, in the "Defining Prevention" section of its strategy, DOD notes that it adopted the CDC's concept that there are three levels of prevention based on when the prevention efforts occur:

- ***Primary Prevention:*** Approaches that take place before sexual violence has occurred to prevent initial perpetration.
- ***Secondary Prevention:*** Immediate responses after sexual violence has occurred to address the early identification of victims and the short-term consequences of violence.
- ***Tertiary Prevention:*** Long-term responses after sexual violence has occurred to address the lasting consequences of violence and sex-offender treatment interventions.

According to DOD, primary prevention is at the core of its focus in developing prevention-related activities, which seek to reduce, with the goal of eliminating factors leading to or associated with, sexual violence, thereby stopping the crime before it occurs. DOD further states that its prevention programs will not rely solely on the training and education of individuals considered to be at risk. Rather, DOD states that its focus on primary prevention will involve empowered and competent individuals interacting in an environment that has been sustained to promote the best possible outcomes.

DOD's strategy also incorporates CDC's concept that there are risk and protective factors that influence the occurrence of sexual violence. According to CDC, identification of risk factors and protective factors is a key step in developing an effective prevention strategy in that it helps to build an understanding of the circumstances—both positive and negative—that may play a role in the perpetration of such incidents. To further enhance the effectiveness of its efforts, CDC categorizes these factors relative to the four domains in which they are identified to exist: (1) society; (2) community; (3) relationship; and (4) individual. According to CDC, this enables an organization to tailor its prevention strategy based on the characteristics of a specific population.

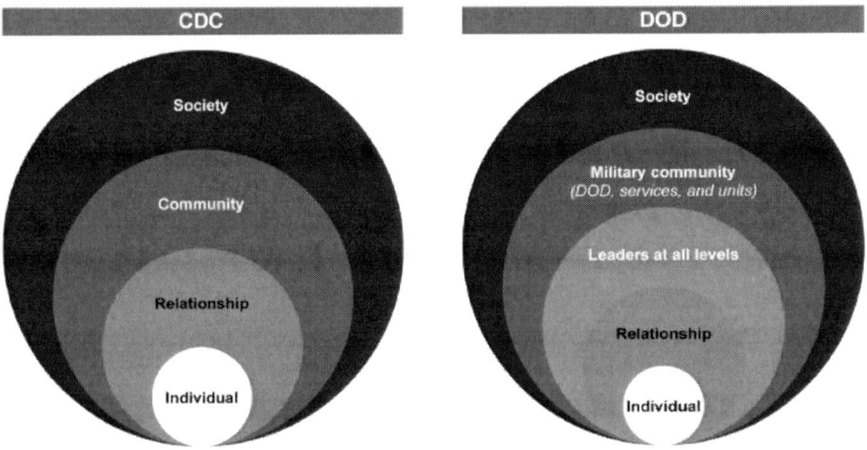

Source: Centers for Disease Control and Prevention (CDC) and Department of Defense (DOD). | GAO-16-61.

Figure 1. CDC's Model of Four Domains in Which Risk and Protective Factors Can Help Target Sexual-Violence Prevention Efforts and DOD's Adaptation of CDC's Model.

In its 2014–16 prevention strategy, DOD adapted CDC's approach by identifying five domains in which it would focus its prevention efforts: (1) society; (2) the military community (DOD/services/units); (3) leaders at all levels; (4) relationships; and (5) individuals.[20] As depicted in figure 1, while DOD's model largely mirrors the one created by CDC, it also included "leaders" as a distinct domain of influence because, according to its 2014–16 strategy, the department wanted to recognize the essential role of leadership and to highlight the necessity that commanders and their staffs develop and execute tactics that target this "center of gravity" for prevention efforts. DOD further notes in its strategy that the inherent complexities of preventing sexual assault necessitates that a number of interventions that span multiple levels must take place to achieve the greatest, and most lasting impact.

DOD's strategy also incorporates key concepts that CDC has identified as being included in the public health approach to prevention. We reviewed DOD's 2014–16 prevention strategy and found that it identifies, and categorizes according to the applicable domain, the four concepts that CDC identified as being included in effective public health strategies, including (1) inputs, (2) activities, (3) outputs, and (4) outcomes. For example, within its society domain, DOD identifies inputs, or the resources on which the effectiveness of an effort depends, such as community volunteers and collaboration with federal partners, coalitions, and other primary prevention experts. In addition, DOD's strategy specifies outputs, which are the direct products of implemented activities and are different from outcomes, which are also included in DOD's strategy and defined as the intended effect of these activities. For example, DOD identifies the development of courses that instruct and empower members as one of the outputs of its efforts, whereas it notes that the establishment and maintenance of a culture that supports the prevention of sexual assault is a desired outcome of its efforts within the "leaders" domain.

DOD's Sexual Assault Prevention Strategy Does Not Link Activities to Desired Outcomes

DOD's strategy identifies 18 prevention-focused activities that it plans to implement as part of its effort to prevent sexual assault, but it does not link these activities to desired outcomes. According to CDC, effective public-health strategies establish a link between activities and their intended outcomes to help determine whether the actual events that take place as part of a program will logically lead to the intended effect.[21] Further, providing a step-by-step roadmap can help identify gaps in program logic that might not otherwise be apparent; persuade skeptics that progress is being made in the right direction, even if the destination has not yet been reached; and aid program managers in identifying what needs to be emphasized right now or what can be done to accelerate progress. In addition to CDC guidance, DOD's Strategic Management Plan for Fiscal Years 2014–2015 identifies the alignment of activities and goals as a key step in achieving desired outcomes.[22] Our prior work on effective agency strategic reviews has also shown that it is important to review progress toward strategic objectives in that it can help to determine subsequent actions, and that leaders and responsible managers should be held accountable for knowing the progress being made in achieving outcomes.[23]

In DOD's 2014–16 prevention strategy, DOD identifies 18 targeted activities, the general time frame in which they are to be accomplished, and the office(s) responsible for their implementation. Specifically, DOD's strategy includes activities such as conducting specialized leader sexual-assault prevention training, establishing collaboration forums to capture and share prevention best practices and lessons learned, and incorporating specific sexual-assault monitoring, measures, and education into normal command training, readiness assessments, and safety forums. In a different section of DOD's strategy, it lists five general outcomes of its prevention efforts such as acceptance and endorsement of the values that seek to prevent sexual assault and an environment in which servicemembers' networks support a culture of sexual-assault prevention. Although both are identified in the strategy, DOD does not discuss what, if any, connection exists between activities and outcomes in the department's efforts to prevent sexual assault.

During our review, we spoke with DOD officials responsible for developing the department's strategy who acknowledged that while it was modeled after CDC's guidance on effective public-health strategies, it did not specify how the activities and outcomes identified in the strategy are linked. According to these officials, the department did not link its prevention activities with outcomes because of a complex interplay that exists between these elements. For example, officials described a scenario in which a single prevention activity could be connected with multiple outcomes. We recognize that such a scenario is possible and believe that it reinforces the importance of understanding how specific activities are expected to contribute to desired outcomes. Thus, without a defined link, DOD may not be able to determine which activities are having the desired effect or, when necessary, to make timely and informed adjustments to its efforts to help ensure it continues to progress toward desired outcomes. Furthermore, DOD may lack the information that is needed to conduct a rigorous evaluation of the effectiveness of its efforts to prevent sexual assault.

DOD's Strategy Does Not Fully Identify Risk and Protective Factors That May Put a Person at Risk for Committing Sexual Assault or, Alternatively, That May Prevent Harm

DOD's strategy is based on CDC's framework for effective sexual-violence prevention strategies, and it addresses some but not all of the elements that CDC identified as necessary to maximize the effectiveness of prevention efforts. According to CDC, there are factors that may put a person at risk for sexual-violence perpetration and victimization while other factors may prevent them from harm. Specifically referred to as risk factors and protective factors, CDC's work has demonstrated that by identifying such influences—relative to the domain or environment in which they exist—organizations can focus their efforts on eliminating factors that promote sexual violence while also supporting the factors that prevent it.[24] In addition to CDC's work on prevention strategies, the Office of Management and Budget issued guidance in 2015 on agencies' strategic reviews in which it acknowledged that while agencies cannot mitigate all risks related to achieving strategic objectives and performance goals, they should identify, measure, and assess challenges related to mission delivery, to the extent possible.[25]

As noted previously, DOD adapted CDC's framework for sexual-violence prevention strategies by identifying five domains to which it would tailor its prevention program, including: (1) society; (2) the military community (DOD/services/units); (3) leaders at all levels; (4) relationships; and (5) individuals. We reviewed DOD's strategy and found that it includes risk factors identified by CDC for three of these domains—individuals, relationships, and society. For example, within the individual risk domain, DOD identified factors such as alcohol and drug use and hostility toward women as risks that may influence sexual violence. Within the relationship domain, DOD identified factors such as associating with sexually aggressive and delinquent peers and having an emotionally unsupportive familial environment as possible influences on the incidence of sexual violence. However, DOD does not specify risk factors for the two domains over which it potentially has the greatest influence—leaders at all levels of DOD and the military community (i.e., DOD/services/units). For example, the strategy does not identify potential risk factors associated with these domains, such as recognizing that the inherent nature of certain types of commands or units may cultivate an environment in which there is an increased risk of sexual assault.

While not specifically tailored to its military-community domain, DOD's prevention strategy includes risk factors that CDC had identified as generally applicable to the community domain. For example, DOD's 2014–16 prevention strategy identifies general tolerance of sexual violence within the community and weak community sanctions against sexual-violence perpetrators as risk factors for that category. While these risk factors may generally apply to DOD, they do not meet CDC's criteria for effective prevention programs because DOD did not identify risk factors and mitigation techniques based on the unique aspects of the military-community domain.

According to officials with DOD SAPRO, they did not identify risk factors specific to DOD's military community and leaders domains because insufficient research existed on risk factors for these domains and the department did not independently take steps to identify relevant risk factors prior to the strategy's publication. A senior DOD official added that DOD asked the RAND Corporation, after the strategy was published, to analyze risk factors, including the military community and leaders domains, as a part of its work on the 2014 Military Workplace Study.[26] In its fiscal year 2014 Department of Defense Annual Report on Sexual Assault in the Military, DOD reported on the findings of RAND's analysis, which included several risk factors for the military-community domain such as differences between service branches as well as between the active-duty and reserve components. RAND did not conduct a similar analysis to identify risk factors for DOD's leader domain.

DOD also included six protective factors identified by CDC in its prevention strategy, but it does not specify how they relate to the five domains. For example, emotional health and connectedness were listed as protective factors for high-school boys that may help to curb the initiation of sexual violence. For high-school girls, academic achievement was listed as a factor that may reduce their exposure to sexual violence. However, the protective factors that DOD included in its strategy are grouped together in a general category rather than being listed under the domain to which they corresponds. During our review, we spoke with a senior DOD official responsible for developing the strategy who acknowledged that more research is needed to identify risk and protective factors for each of the domains in its model. Without a more comprehensive list of such factors that correspond to each of the domains in its strategy, DOD may be limited in its ability to take an evidence-based approach to the prevention of sexual assault. Further, DOD may not be able to accurately characterize the environment in which sexual assaults occur or to develop activities and interventions to more effectively prevent them. Table 1 provides additional details about the risk factors identified by domain in DOD's 2014-16 Sexual Assault Prevention Strategy.

Table 1. Risk Factors[a] Identified in the Department of Defense's (DOD) 2014-16 Sexual Assault Prevention Strategy By Domain

Individual	Relationship	Leaders at all levels	DOD/ services/units	Society
•Alcohol and drug use •Coercive sexual fantasies •Impulsive and antisocial tendencies •Preference for impersonal sex •Hostility towards women •Hypermasculinity •Childhood history of sexual and physical abuse •Witnessed family violence as a child	•Association with sexually aggressive and delinquent peers •Family environment characterized by physical violence and few resources •Strong patriarchal relationship or familial environment •Emotionally unsupportive familial environment	Not included	Not included	•Poverty •Societal norms that support sexualviolence •Societal norms that support male superiority and sexual entitlement •Societal norms that maintain women's inferiority and sexual submissiveness •Weak laws and policies related to gender equity •High tolerance levels of crime and other forms of violence

Source: GAO analysis of DOD data. | GAO-16-61

Note: Data are from DOD's 2014-16 Sexual Assault Prevention Strategy (Apr. 30, 2014).

[a]DOD also included the following six protective factors in its strategy: (1) Emotional health and connectedness (high-school boys); (2) Academic achievement (high-school girls); (3) "Loss of face"— a concern for how one's actions affect others (among Asian American men); (4) Parent's use of reasoning to resolve family conflicts (males); (5) Effect varied by risk factor; and (6) Empathy had several direct and indirect effects. However, DOD did not specify how they relate to the five domains.

DOD and the Services Are Implementing Prevention Activities but They Have Not Taken Steps to Help Ensure That Installation-Developed Activities Are Consistent with the Objectives of DOD's Prevention Strategy

DOD and the military services developed and are in the process of implementing prevention-focused activities, but they have not taken steps to help ensure that activities developed at the local level are consistent with the overarching objectives of DOD's strategy. As noted previously, DOD's 2014–16 prevention strategy identifies 18 prevention-focused activities and, according to SAPRO officials, 2 have been implemented and efforts to address the remaining 16 are ongoing. In addition to the activities listed in DOD's strategy, installation-based personnel have developed and implemented various prevention activities at military-service installations. However, these installation-developed activities may not be consistent with DOD's prevention strategy because DOD and the services have not communicated the purpose of the strategy and disseminated it to the installation-based personnel responsible for developing and implementing activities at the local level. Further, the military services' SAPR policies—key conduits of such communication—have not been updated to align with the guidance in the strategy. During visits to selected installations, we also found that there is limited collaboration taking place on the prevention activities developed locally, which could further affect the effectiveness and efficiency of the department's efforts to prevent sexual assault within the military.

DOD's Implementation of Most Activities in Its Prevention Strategy Are Ongoing

DOD and the military services are in the process of implementing the prevention-focused activities noted in DOD's 2014-16 Sexual Assault Prevention Strategy. In its strategy, DOD specifies that one of the department's goals is to deliver consistent and effective sexual-assault prevention methods and programs. In doing so, DOD believes that it will help to instill a culture of mutual respect and trust, professional values, and team commitment, which are reinforced to create an environment where sexual assault is not tolerated, condoned, or ignored. To achieve this goal, DOD identified 18 activities in its prevention strategy as well as their general time frame for completion, their priority relative to the overall strategy, and the office with primary responsibility for their implementation (i.e., SAPRO, military department, or service).[27] For example, one activity assigns SAPRO responsibility for developing a military community of practice focused on primary prevention within 1 year of the strategy's April 2014 publication. Other activities, such as implementing policies that appropriately address high-risk situations targeted by offenders are designated as responsibilities of the military services and are to be completed within 3 years of the strategy's implementation. Table 2 provides a comprehensive list of the 18 prevention-focused activities identified in DOD's 2014-16 Sexual Assault Prevention Strategy as well as the time frames in which they are to be implemented and the offices responsible for their implementation.

Table 2. Prevention-Focused Activities Identified in the Department of Defense's (DOD) 2014-16 Sexual Assault Prevention Strategy Published in April 2014

Activity	Implementation timeline[a]	Implementation responsibility
Implement the 2014-16 Sexual Assault Prevention Strategy.	Short	All
Conduct specialized leader sexual-assault prevention training.	Short	Military departments and services
Develop and expand gender-responsive and culturally competent programs to address healthy relationships and active bystander intervention with the emphasis that core values should anchor all actions in order to support the establishment of a culture of mutual respect.	Short	Military departments and services
Review and if necessary expand DOD and service alcohol policies to address factors beyond individual use.	Short	Military departments and services
Develop a process for command review of information on sex-related offenses in personnel service records of members of the Armed Forces (for purpose of reducing likelihood that repeat offenses will escape notice) in accordance with section 1745 of the National Defense Authorization Act for Fiscal Year 2014.	Short	Military departments and services
Explore the development of and the enhancement of existing sexual-assault deterrence measures and messaging (e.g., publishing court-martial results).	Medium	Military departments and services, DOD's Sexual Assault Prevention and Response Office (SAPRO)

Table 2. (Continued)

Activity	Implementation timeline[a]	Implementation responsibility
Assess, implement core competencies, and continue to update all sexual-assault prevention–related training and programs based on latest evidence-based research, practices, and lessons learned.	Continual	Military departments and services, SAPRO
Implement policies that appropriately address high-risk situations targeted by offenders.	Long	Military departments and services
Institute recurring senior leadership meetings (e.g., leader summits) to review sexual-assault prevention programs (not case-management group meetings).	Medium	Military departments and services
Identify and implement incentives for the prevention of sexual assault and other related behaviors (e.g., alcohol abuse, sexual harassment, hazing).	Long	Military departments and services, SAPRO
Develop a military community of practice focused on primary prevention of sexual assault.	Short	SAPRO
Establish collaboration forums with external experts, federal partners, military services, advocacy organizations, and educational institutions to capture and share prevention best practices and lessons learned in accordance with federal law and department regulations.	Continual	Military departments and services, SAPRO
Develop a prevention guide that outlines promising practices and lessons learned in sexual-assault prevention.	Short	SAPRO
Review national (e.g., state, university), and coalition (e.g., United Kingdom and Canada) sexual-assault prevention programs to identify best practices and lessons learned.	Continual	SAPRO
Develop sexual-assault prevention strategies and programs that employ peers, near-peers (i.e., servicemember one rank higher or somewhat senior in position of authority), and social influencers.	Continual	Military departments and services

Activity	Implementation timeline[a]	Implementation responsibility
Incorporate specific sexual-assault monitoring, measures, and education into normal command training, readiness assessments, and safety forums.	Continual	Military departments and services
Assess transition policies that ensure servicemember sponsorship, unit integration, and immediate assignment into a chain of command.	Continual	Military departments and services
Identify and implement sexual-assault prevention tools (e.g., mobile apps, leader toolkits).	Medium	SAPRO

Source: DOD. | GAO-16-61

Note: Data are from DOD's 2014-16 Sexual Assault Prevention Strategy.

[a]In its 2014-16 Sexual Assault Prevention Strategy, DOD specified that each activity would be implemented according to one of four designated time frames that started on the date of the strategy's publication (April 2014): Short = 0 to 1 year; Medium = 1 to 2 years; Long = 2 to 3 years; and Continual = ongoing/cyclic requirement.

According to SAPRO, the office responsible for developing the department's strategy, 2 of the 18 activities identified in the strategy have been fully implemented. Specifically, SAPRO officials said its activities "Implementation of the 2014-16 Sexual Assault Prevention Strategy" and "Develop a military community of practice focused on primary prevention of sexual assault" are complete and the remaining 16 activities are ongoing. Officials stated that the implementation of the 2014-16 Sexual Assault Prevention Strategy activity was completed with its publication in April 2014. SAPRO also noted that a military community of practice was started with the August 2014 implementation of "SAPR Connect"—an online community in which DOD SAPR personnel can collaborate and share ideas, news, research, and insights from experts on issues related to sexual assault.

In addition to the 2 activities it identified as implemented, efforts are under way to implement the remaining 16. However, SAPRO officials said that the remaining 16 activities identified in its strategy will never be considered "complete" because, as the program develops, the department will consistently revise and renew its approach in these areas. As such, officials stated that the status of the remaining 16 activities is, and will indefinitely remain, designated as "ongoing." Though the remaining activities are not considered complete, each service has taken steps to support the ongoing efforts specified in the department's strategy. For example, each military service annually administers sexual-assault prevention and response training that addresses the nature of sexual assault in the military environment using scenario-based, real-life situations to demonstrate the entire cycle of prevention, reporting, response, and accountability procedures. In addition, each service has developed and implemented its own prevention-focused training. For example, in the spring of 2014, the Air Force held a SAPR Stand-Down Day focused on teaching airmen to identify sexual-assault offenders by showing how they operate and to impart the effect that offenders can have on their victims. In 2014, the Marine Corps also expanded its SAPR training efforts to include courses that emphasize character, social courage, and mutual respect among Marines. Specifically, the Marine Corps instituted a 2-hour ethics course of instruction for new recruits who are awaiting travel to their initial military training, which focuses on developing an understanding of sexual assault, harassment, hazing, and alcohol abuse.[28]

The services have also taken steps to address the activity that directs them to review and, if necessary, expand alcohol policies to address factors beyond individual use. For example, some Army installations have adopted more stringent alcohol policies, such as limiting the amount of alcohol that soldiers may have in the barracks or purchase from installation facilities, and the Navy took steps to improve its training of alcohol providers and to engage local-community leadership and organizations to expand prevention efforts off base. In addition, the Marine Corps restricted on-base retail alcoholic beverage sales to the hours of 8:00 a.m. to 10:00 p.m. and limited its availability in non–package stores to no more than 10 percent of the total retail selling floor space, while the Air Force revised its alcoholic beverage policy to deglamorize behavior associated with excessive drinking.

The Services Have Implemented Installation-Developed Prevention Activities Even Though DOD's Prevention Strategy Has Not Been Thoroughly Communicated or Disseminated

The military services have developed and implemented activities at the installation level, independent of DOD's prevention strategy, in an effort to prevent sexual assault. DOD acknowledged that the 18 activities in the 2014–16 prevention strategy are not the only required prevention activities and encouraged the services to develop their own specific activities. However, DOD also noted that the objectives of DOD's prevention strategy are to achieve unity of effort and purpose across all of DOD in the execution of sexual-assault prevention. During our visits to selected installations, we found that program personnel were largely unfamiliar with DOD's prevention strategy and hence may not be implementing activities in a manner consistent with the objectives of DOD's strategy. In its 2014-16 prevention strategy, DOD highlights that it is important for leaders to employ targeted interventions, standards, and messaging to address issues unique to their unit climate, and that prevention programs should be tailored to specific audiences and for specific purposes and circumstances. However, DOD also notes that the strategy provides a framework, means, ways, and supporting end states to assist leaders and planners in the development of appropriate activities. SAPRO officials stated that they have implemented several initiatives to communicate directly with the SAPR Program Leads on prevention strategy as well as servicemembers in the field. For example, as of October 1, 2015 SAPRO has provided workshops to SARCs from the Navy and Marine Corps on implementation of the prevention strategy via webinar or face-to-face to help participants translate the strategy into action. Other workshops' dates are being finalized.

During the course of our review, we met with military officials and program personnel from a joint base and three service-specific installations who described prevention activities that had been developed locally and were not listed in DOD's strategy. The efforts at these installations included a variety of activities ranging from displays of sexual-assault awareness symbols to service-sponsored sporting events that were generally based on the theme of preventing sexual assault. Despite their responsibilities for and experience with coordinating and implementing prevention-focused activities, the program personnel we met with consistently said that DOD and their respective services had not communicated and disseminated guidance to them on the department's prevention strategy and that they were generally unaware of how the department's 2014–16 prevention strategy related to their development and implementation of sexual-assault prevention activities.

In the absence of such guidance, we discussed with SAPR personnel at the installations we visited their processes for determining which prevention-focused activities to sponsor. For example, we spoke with program personnel at one installation who said that while they were aware of DOD's prevention strategy, they had not received any headquarter-level guidance or direction on the types of activities they should sponsor in support of their efforts to prevent sexual assault. At another installation, we spoke with program personnel who stated they didn't think that the communication flow between the headquarters-level SAPR office and the installation was as fast or as formal as it needs to be to address a constantly changing program. In addition, SAPR personnel provided a briefing on their program in which prevention-focused activities were categorized according to the five domains identified in DOD's 2014- 16 prevention strategy. When we asked how they became familiar with DOD's prevention strategy, a program official said she had found the information during a self-initiated search through documents on SAPRO's website. Such an action is noteworthy; however, without a plan to communicate the prevention strategy and roles and responsibilities for its implementation, DOD and the military services cannot be sure that all installation-based program personnel are implementing activities that are designed to achieve the goals and objectives of the department's prevention strategy.

We also found that the services' SAPR policies—a key conduit for communicating a program's purpose and corresponding roles and responsibilities to relevant personnel—have not been updated to reflect the tenets of DOD's most recent prevention strategy. DOD's 2014-16 Sexual Assault Prevention Strategy specifies that one of the department's objectives is to achieve unity of effort and purpose across all of DOD in the execution of sexual-assault prevention and also directs the DOD components and the Secretaries of the military departments to align their implementing plans and policies with the department's prevention strategy. While the services' SAPR policies generally address the prevention of sexual assault, they have not been updated to align with and operationalize the principles outlined in DOD's most recent prevention strategy. Specifically, the Army and Air Force have revised their policies after the issuance of DOD's 2014–16 prevention strategy, but neither incorporates specific elements of DOD's prevention strategy. The Navy and Marine Corps SAPR policies were issued in 2013 prior to the issuance of DOD's 2014–2016 prevention strategy and have yet to be updated.[29].

We recognize that DOD's most recent prevention strategy was published approximately a year and a half ago and that it takes time for its prevention strategy to take root in an organization as large as DOD. However, there may be a disconnect between DOD's SAPR policies and what is being implemented by the services—something that has previously been identified within the department as a challenge. Notably, in May 2012, the Joint Chiefs of Staff issued its Strategic Direction to the Joint Force on Sexual Assault Prevention and Response in which it noted that evidence clearly indicated that gaps remain between the precepts of the DOD's SAPR program and its full implementation at command and unit levels.[30] Thus, without SAPR policies that are aligned with the department's prevention strategy, the military services will be limited in their ability to promote consistency in the prevention efforts that are being developed and implemented throughout DOD.

Challenges Identified in Cross-Service Collaboration at Selected Sites

During site visits to a joint base and three service-specific installations in the same geographic location, we found limited collaboration among the services on their efforts to prevent sexual assault. DOD's 2014-16 Sexual Assault Prevention Strategy directs the military services to collaborate so they can capture and share best practices and lessons learned related to the prevention of sexual assault. This direction is further reinforced in both the 2013 and 2015 versions of its SAPR strategic plan, which note that it is the department's objective to deliver consistent and effective prevention methods and programs. Further, the May 2012 Strategic Direction from the Joint Chiefs of Staff, which predates DOD's current prevention strategy, directed commanders and leaders across the military services to synchronize their respective sexual-assault prevention and response programs to increase unity of effort through a joint perspective and consistent application of prevention, intervention, and response.

During our site visits, we met with military officials and SAPR program personnel who consistently acknowledged the need to improve cross-service collaboration on the prevention of sexual assault. However, they added that the different structures and processes of their respective services' SAPR programs complicated such collaboration. For example, during a visit to an Army base, program personnel informed us of an attempt to collaborate with the other services on SAPR activities. However, they added that the other services declined to collaborate because the other services, whose programs were solely focused on addressing sexual assault, thought it would be confusing to collaborate with the Army since their program now addressed both sexual harassment and assault.[31] During a visit to another installation, a military official stated that the extent of cross-service collaboration on SAPR is based on the individuals involved and the level of importance that they place on pursuing joint activities. The official added that he was not aware of any overarching headquarters-level guidance that promoted such collaboration when the cross-service relationship and desire to work together did not exist.

In addition to the structural differences of each service, program personnel said that they do not have the number of personnel needed to cultivate more cross-service SAPR activities. Specifically, program personnel said that their SAPR offices were consistently understaffed and that the staff who are available are focused on the needs of their respective service's program. For example, we met with SAPR personnel at one installation who said that there is one SARC and one victim advocate assigned to serve a population of 1,200 servicemembers. Additionally, SAPR personnel from another installation said that it can be difficult to maintain a sufficient number of SAPR personnel because many of their staff and volunteers are servicemembers who become unavailable, and in some cases, not replaced when they deploy.

During the course of our review, we met with headquarters-level officials in SAPRO who explained that, during joint-base negotiations, the services decided that SAPR programs would remain separate. Specifically, SAPRO officials said that while the Army has made an effort to develop joint response centers, all of the military services wanted procedures, such as sexual-assault investigations, to be handled by their respective service. SAPRO officials stated, however, that one of the assessment tasks in its strategic plan is to conduct a review of joint environments and that they have added questions on joint basing for the military services to respond to and include as part of their input to DOD's Annual Report on Sexual Assault in the Military.

DOD Has Identified Prevention-Focused Measures, but They Are Missing Some Key Attributes Needed to Successfully Assess Program Performance

DOD has identified performance measures to assess the extent to which its prevention efforts are achieving its goal to eliminate sexual assault in the military, but these measures are missing many of the 10 key attributes that our prior work has shown can contribute to assessing program performance effectively. Specifically, DOD has identified 12 performance measures that it will use to assess the overall effectiveness of its sexual-assault prevention and response program, and 5 of these measures are specifically designed to gauge the effectiveness of its prevention line of effort. While all 5 of DOD's prevention-focused measures demonstrate some of the key attributes, collectively they are missing more than half of these attributes.

DOD Has Identified Performance Measures to Assess Its Efforts to Prevent Sexual Assault

DOD has recently identified a new set of performance measures to assess its efforts to prevent sexual assault. Since 2005, DOD's SAPR policy has required that the Under Secretary of Defense for Personnel and Readiness develop metrics to measure compliance and effectiveness of training, awareness, prevention, and response policies and programs.[32] Since that time, we have recommended, among other things, that DOD develop an oversight framework that contained performance goals, strategies to be used to accomplish goals, and criteria to measure the progress of its prevention and response efforts.[33] In October 2009, Congress required DOD to submit a revised SAPR implementation plan to include, among other things, methods to measure the effectiveness of plans that implement DOD policies regarding sexual assaults involving members of the armed forces.[34] In response, in April 2010, DOD conceptualized several measures and further directed in its 2013 SAPR strategic plan that they be developed. In its Annual Report on Sexual Assault in the Military Services for Fiscal Year 2013, DOD identified six performance measures, referred to as SAPR Metrics 1.0, that had been developed to measure the effectiveness of its SAPR program. However, none of the six performance measures were developed specifically to assess DOD's progress toward preventing sexual assault.

More recently, the President directed the Secretary of Defense to develop a comprehensive report on major improvements to DOD's SAPR program since August 2013 and to identify clear benchmarks and metrics that will enable the department to measure the effectiveness of its SAPR efforts. In response to this direction, DOD collaborated with the White House and identified 12 performance measures[35] that the department plans to use to assess the effectiveness of its SAPR program and that were included in DOD's November 2014 report to the President.[36] Of the 12 performance measures, 5 were designed to specifically measure the effectiveness of DOD's prevention line of effort.[37] Table 3 further describes DOD's 5 prevention-focused performance measures.

Table 3. DOD's Prevention-Focused Performance Measures

Performance measure	Description
Past-Year Prevalence of Unwanted Sexual Contact	Measures the estimated past-year prevalence of unwanted sexual contact and sexual assault and estimated number of servicemembers experiencing unwanted sexual contact and sexual assault, as indicated by the Department of Defense's (DOD) Workplace and Gender Relations Survey of Active Duty Members surveys and RAND's Military Workplace Study survey.
Prevalence versus Reporting	Measures the estimated number of servicemembers who have experienced sexual assaultand have not reported it by measuring the difference between the estimated number of servicemembers who have experienced unwanted sexual contact, as calculated with data from the Workplace and Gender Relations Survey of Active Duty Members surveys, and the number of servicemember victims in sexual-assault reports for incidents occurring during military service.
Bystander Intervention Experience in the Past Year	Measures servicemember responses to DOD's Defense Equal Opportunity Management Institute Organizational Climate Survey (DEOCS) question: "In the past 12 months, I observed a situation that I believed was, or could have led to, a sexual assault" and, if servicemembers observed a high-risk situation, whether or not they intervened.
Command Climate Index—Addressing Continuum of Harm	Measures servicemember perceptions of the extent to which their leadership promotes a climate based on mutual respect and trust. Specifically, measures servicemember responses to DOD's DEOCS questions: "To what extent does your chain of command: (1) Promote a unit climate based on "respect and trust"? (2) Refrain from sexist comments and behaviors? (3) Actively discourage sexist comments and behaviors?"
Perceptions of Leadership Support for SAPR	Measures servicemember perceptions of command and leadership support for Sexual Assault Prevention and Response (SAPR) programs. Specifically, measures servicemember response to DOD's DEOCS questions: "To what extent does your chain of command: (1) Encourage victims to report sexual assault? (2) Create an environment where victims feel comfortable reporting sexual assault?"

Source: GAO analysis of DOD data. | GAO-16-61

Note: Data are from DOD's November 2014 report to the President.

DOD's Prevention-Focused Measures Are Missing Many of the 10 Attributes That Contribute to Assessing Program Performance

We analyzed DOD's five prevention-focused measures and found that they are missing many of the 10 key attributes that contribute to assessing program performance effectively.[38] Our prior work has shown that agencies successful in measuring performance used measures that demonstrated results, were limited to the vital few, covered multiple priorities, and provided information that was useful for decision making.[39] To determine whether DOD's prevention-focused performance measures satisfy these four general characteristics, we assessed the measures using 10 specific attributes.[40] Our work cited these specific attributes as key to successful performance measures.[41] Table 4 shows the 10 attributes, their definitions, and the potentially adverse consequences of not having the attributes.

Table 4. GAO's Key Attributes of Successful Performance Measures

Attribute	Definition	Potentially adverse consequences of notmeeting attribute
Key attributes evaluated by reviewing performance measures individually		
Linkage	Measure is aligned with division and agency-wide goals and mission and clearly communicated throughout the organization.	Behaviors and incentives created by measures do not support achieving division or agency-wide goals or mission.
Baseline and Trend Data	Measure has a baseline and trend data associated with it to identify, monitor, and report changes in performance and to help ensure that performance is viewed in context.	Without adequate baseline data, goals may not permit subsequent comparison with actual performance.
Measurable target	Measure has a numerical goal.	Cannot tell whether performance is meetingexpectations.
Clarity	Measure is clearly stated, and the name and definition are consistent with the methodology used to calculate it.	Data could be confusing and misleading to users.
Objectivity	Measure is reasonably free from significant bias or manipulation.	Performance assessments may be systematically over- or understated.
Reliability	Measure produces the same result under similar conditions.	Reported performance data are inconsistent and add uncertainty.

Table 4. (Continued)

Attribute	Definition	Potentially adverse consequences of notmeeting attribute
Key attributes evaluated by reviewing performance measures as a set		
Limited overlap	Measure should provide new information beyond that provided by other measures.	Managers may have to sort through redundant, costly information that does not add value.
Core program activities	Measures cover the activities that an entity is expected to perform to support the intent of the program.	Not enough information availablein core program areas to managers and stakeholders.
Government-wide priorities	Each measure should cover a priority, such as quality, timeliness, and cost of service.	A program's overall success is at risk if all priorities are not addressed.
Balance	Balance exists when a suite of measures ensures that an organization's various priorities are covered.	Lack of balance could create skewed incentives when measures overemphasize some goals.

Source: GAO. | GAO-16-61

Our analysis determined that all five of DOD's prevention-focused performance measures demonstrate some of the key attributes, but collectively they are missing more than half of the key attributes of successful performance measures that we identified in our prior work. Specifically, DOD's performance measures have **linkage** in that they are aligned with the prevention line of effort set forth in DOD's 2014–16 prevention strategy, include **baseline and trend data**, and exhibit **little to no overlap with other measures**. We also found, however, that DOD's prevention-focused performance measures' usefulness to the department may be limited because they each do not have between 5 and 7 of the 10 key attributes that we identified as necessary to successfully measure program performance. Table 5 shows the results of our evaluation of DOD's prevention-focused performance measures using the 10 key attributes of successful performance measures.

Table 5. Comparison of DOD's Prevention-Focused Performance Measures to GAO's Key Attributes of Successful Performance Measures

These attributes apply to the measures individually							These attributes apply to the overall suite of measures rather than to the measures individually			
Prevention-focused performance measure	Linkage	Baseline and trend data	Measurable target	Clarity	Objectivity	Reliability	Limited overlap	Core program activities	Government-wide priorities	Balance
Past-Year Prevalence of Unwanted Sexual Contact	√	√			√	√	√			
Prevalence versus Reporting	√	√			√	√	√			
Bystander Intervention Experience in the Past Year	√	√					√			
Command Climate Index— Addressing Continuum of Harm	√	√					√			
Perceptions of Leadership Support for Sexual Assault Prevention and Response	√	√					√			

Source: GAO analysis of Department of Defense (DOD) data. | GAO-16-61

As shown in table 5, all of DOD's prevention-focused performance measures are missing the attribute of measurable targets. Leading practices in federal agency performance management state that, where appropriate, performance measures should have quantifiable, numerical targets and that agencies could use baselines to set realistic but challenging targets. As noted previously, DOD has established baseline and trend data for each of its prevention-focused performance measures, but none of these measures have **measurable targets** because it has not used these data to set numerical goals nor has it provided the information needed to appropriately interpret the results of the measures and determine program achievements. For example, for its "Prevalence versus Reporting" measure, while DOD has expressed that it aims to close the gap by decreasing the prevalence of sexual-assault incidents and increasing the number of victims willing to report a sexual assault, it does not identify—in either case—a numerical target for the department to work towards. DOD officials told us that the department has not established numerical targets for its prevention-focused performance measures, because it instead uses indicators such as positive results from surveys or a decrease in the sexual-assault prevalence rate when compared to previous years as measures of success. Further, officials stated they have not established numerical targets because there is not enough research to determine what an appropriate target should be for its measures related to prevalence.

We recognize the challenges associated with measuring the progress of activities with complex outcomes and limited examples to replicate, such as DOD's efforts to prevent sexual assault. In these instances, our prior work on effective agency strategic reviews has shown that setting measurable targets is an evolutionary process involving trial and error and that agencies may need to break their strategic objectives into pieces that can be more easily be measured or assessed. Further, for activities with long-term, scientific discovery–oriented outcomes, agencies can also rely on underlying multiyear performance goals, annual performance indicators, and milestones to better plan for and understand near-term progress towards those objectives.[42] Without a numerical target, DOD and other decision makers may be unable to gauge the extent of progress from the department's prevention efforts because there are no goals that can be used to compare projected performance with actual results. Furthermore, without targets against which it can measure its progress, DOD may not be able to ensure that it is allocating resources to its most effective activities—a key determination given the increasingly limited fiscal resources across the federal government.

Our analysis also determined that all five of DOD's prevention-focused performance measures are missing the attribute of **clarity** because the corresponding methodology is not clearly defined. For example, DOD did not specify that it would assess program performance by gender or rank; however, we found that three of DOD's five prevention-focused performance measures assessed performance both by gender and by rank, while another was focused solely on results broken out by servicemember gender. According to a senior official, DOD chooses to measure performance by gender and rank because data show that women and junior enlisted servicemembers in general are at higher risk of sexual assault. However, DOD did not use gender or rank when calculating its "Prevalence versus Reporting" measure. In our March 2015 report focusing on male-servicemember sexual-assault victims, we reported that developing clear goals and associated metrics related to male victims and articulating them throughout the department would provide DOD with additional information to assess its progress and determine whether any adjustments are needed in its approach for addressing sexual assault in the military.[43] Similarly, DOD would benefit in developing clear goals and associated performance measures by gender and rank so it can effectively assess its progress of preventing sexual assaults from occurring in the military.

Further, DOD's Prevalence versus reporting measure is not clearly defined. Specifically, the measure's name and definition suggests that the department intends to compare the estimated prevalence of unwanted sexual contact with the number of sexual assaults reported by servicemembers while serving in the military by fiscal year. However, DOD's annual data on sexual-assault incidents reported to the military services by fiscal year include assaults that occurred prior to the fiscal year in which they were reported. As a result, DOD is comparing the prevalence of unwanted sexual contact that occurred in the past year to reported sexual assaults, regardless of when they occurred. Given the lack of available data on the fiscal year in which the sexual-assault incidents occurred, we are unable to accurately compare the prevalence of unwanted sexual contact to reported sexual assault by fiscal year. However, our analysis of DOD's annual reports since fiscal year 2008 shows an increase in the percentage of unrestricted reports of sexual assault made for an incident that occurred prior to the fiscal year it was reported, with about 12 percent reporting a prior-year incident in fiscal year 2008 compared to at least 24 percent reporting a prior-year incident in fiscal year 2013. The lack of clarity of what actually is being measured may lead decision makers to believe that performance was better or worse than it actually was.

Our analysis also determined that **objectivity** and **reliability** may be limited for three of the five prevention-focused performance measures, because they are based on the results of a convenience sample[44] of servicemembers who respond to the Defense Equal Opportunity Management Institute (DEOMI) Organizational Climate Survey request and voluntarily complete the command-climate survey. As such, the aggregated results are not generalizable to the larger servicemember population. According to a senior DOD official, DOD is still determining the usefulness of using the command-climate survey at the department level by exploring ways to make the results more representative and meaningful at the department level. Performance measures lacking objectivity and reliability may affect the conclusions about the extent to which progress has been made.

Additionally, our analysis determined that DOD's overall suite of prevention-focused performance measures does not identify **core program activities** that relate to its prevention efforts, does not address **government-wide priorities** such as cost, quality, and timeliness, and, as a result, is not **balanced** among priorities. For example, DOD identifies SAPR education and training as a key component of its prevention program, but it is unclear how DOD will determine their effectiveness given that none of DOD's measures are designed to gauge the effectiveness of such activities. Senior DOD officials acknowledged that DOD has more work to do on refining its sexual-assault prevention metrics. However, until DOD has fully developed its prevention-focused performance measures, DOD and other decision makers may be unable to effectively gauge the progress of the department's prevention efforts.

CONCLUSION

Since our first report in 2008 on sexual assault in the military, DOD has made progress in improving its efforts to prevent and respond to sexual assault across the department. For example, to further develop its strategy to prevent sexual assault, DOD consulted with CDC and incorporated CDC's framework and prevention-related concepts into its prevention strategy. This included, among other things, defining the different levels at which sexual-assault prevention efforts occur and describing the importance of identifying and understanding the domains in which sexual violence takes place. However, DOD's 2014-16 Prevention Strategy does not provide a linkage between its prevention-focused activities and their desired outcomes and it does not identify risk factors for two of its domains. These actions could help DOD ensure that it is taking an evidence-based approach to the prevention of sexual assault. Further, the prevention strategy has not been systematically communicated or disseminated to the installation-based program personnel responsible for its implementation, and the services' SAPR policies—another means for communicating direction to program personnel—have not been aligned with the strategy to reinforce its purpose. Finally, while DOD has identified performance measures, the measures are not, in all cases, in line with the key attributes of successful performance measures, which make it difficult for the department to reliably determine which activities are helping to prevent sexual assault. Without fully developing its strategy to prevent sexual assault by linking prevention activities to desired outcomes, identifying risk factors for all domains, and including fully developed performance measures, leadership at all levels of DOD may face challenges in determining the best prevention efforts to implement in order to prevent sexual assault. Further, without communicating, disseminating, and aligning the department's overarching strategy to prevent sexual assault with the installation level of the military services, DOD could encounter difficulties in carrying out its vision to eliminate sexual assault in the military. Lastly, at the three service-specific and one joint installation we visited, we found challenges related to collaboration in implementing sexual-assault prevention activities across the services. While this may not be indicative of all service-specific or joint installations, it may require DOD's attention in the future.

Recommendations for Executive Action

To improve the effectiveness of DOD's strategy for preventing sexual assault in the military, we recommend that, as part of the department's next biennial update to the 2014–16 sexual-assault prevention strategy, the Secretary of Defense direct the Under Secretary of Defense for Personnel and Readiness, in conjunction with the Secretaries of the military departments, take the following five actions:

- link sexual-assault prevention activities with desired outcomes, and
- identify risk and protective factors for all of its domains, including the military community and its leaders.

To help ensure widespread adoption and implementation of DOD's sexual-assault prevention strategy and to fulfill its role as a framework that can assist leaders and planners in the development of appropriate tasks, we recommend that the Secretary of Defense direct the Under Secretary of Defense for Personnel and Readiness, in conjunction with the Secretaries of the military departments, to

- communicate and disseminate DOD's prevention strategy and its purpose to the appropriate levels of program personnel as well as their roles and responsibilities for its implementation, and
- ensure the military services' SAPR policies are aligned with the department's prevention strategy.

To help improve DOD's ability to measure the effectiveness of the department's efforts in preventing sexual assault in the military, we recommend that the Secretary of Defense direct the Under Secretary of Defense for Personnel and Readiness, in collaboration with the Secretaries of the military departments, to fully develop the department's performance measures for the prevention of sexual assault so that the measures include all key attributes of successful performance measures.

Agency Comments and Our Evaluation

In written comments on a draft of this report, DOD concurred with each of our five recommendations. DOD's comments are summarized below. DOD also provided technical comments on the draft report, which we incorporated as appropriate.

DOD concurred with our first and second recommendations that seek to improve the effectiveness of the department's strategy for preventing sexual assault by linking sexual assault prevention activities with desired outcomes and identifying risk and protective factors for all of its domains, including the military community and its leaders. In its comments, DOD agreed that linking prevention activities to desired outcomes is important and stated that it had developed a methodology to identify the full range of risk and protective factors for the five domains in which it will focus its efforts to prevent sexual assault. DOD also stated that in future phases of the study, it will attempt to link future prevention activities with changes in indicators for risk and protective factors as well as the occurrence of sexual assault. We are encouraged by the efforts DOD has underway to more comprehensively identify risk and protective factors and believe that these efforts will better position the department to focus on eliminating factors that promote sexual assault and to support the factors that may prevent it.

Regarding the implementation of DOD's prevention strategy and its use as a framework to develop appropriate tasks, DOD concurred with our third and fourth recommendations that it communicate and disseminate the prevention strategy and its purpose to the appropriate levels of program personnel as well as their roles and responsibilities for its implementation, and ensure the military services' SAPR policies are aligned with the department's prevention strategy. In its comments, DOD identified several efforts that it had initiated related to the communication and implementation of its sexual assault prevention strategy. For example, DOD described a prevention roundtable that includes representatives from the military services, the National Guard Bureau, and the Coast Guard and meets quarterly to collaborate on sexual assault prevention requirements and to share their efforts to prevent sexual assault. DOD also highlighted that, for more than 2 years, it has hosted quarterly webinars on topics that can assist with the implementation of its prevention strategy. We are encouraged by the variety of forums that DOD sponsors to facilitate information-sharing on prevention initiatives and, in particular, its recent institution of workshops that help participants to operationalize the prevention strategy. However, as we noted in our report, it is important for DOD to develop a plan for communicating the prevention strategy and its purpose to all personnel to help ensure that it achieves its goal of department-wide unity of effort in the prevention of sexual assault.

With regard to the department's ability to measure the effectiveness of its efforts to prevent sexual assault, DOD concurred with our fifth recommendation that it fully develop its performance measures for the prevention of sexual assault so that they include all key attributes of successful performance measures. In its comments, DOD stated that CDC and leading researchers have recognized sexual assault is a nonstandard public health issue that requires different metrics to determine the causal linkages that exist between preventive indicators and prevention-related outcomes. DOD also stated that it would continue to monitor best practices in civilian prevention initiatives, and translate them to military populations as appropriate. As noted in our report, we recognize the challenges associated with measuring the progress of activities with complex outcomes, such as DOD's efforts to prevent sexual assault. In these instances, our prior work on effective agency strategic reviews has shown that the development of performance measures is an evolutionary process that involves trial and error, particularly for activities with long-term, scientific discovery-oriented outcomes such as the prevention of sexual assault. We also recognize the difficulties that are posed to emergent initiatives—such as the prevention of sexual assault in the military—by the limited number of examples from civilian initiatives that may exist to be replicated. However, given the substantive differences between military and civilian culture, we encourage DOD to pioneer measures that will most effectively depict the department's performance.

Brenda S. Farrell
Director,
Defense Capabilities and Management

Appendix I: Prevention-Focused Program Improvements since 2013 That DOD Highlighted in Its November 2014 Report to the President

In a December 2013 letter, the President of the United States directed the Secretary of Defense to provide a comprehensive report—by the following December—on the Department of Defense's (DOD) progress in addressing the issue of sexual assault. Specifically, the report was to address major programmatic improvements made by DOD since August 2013, including those related to the prevention of sexual assault.[1] Accordingly, in November 2014, DOD submitted its report to the President in which it noted that the department had increased its focus on prevention and had demonstrated progress in preventing sexual assault, and that it planned to intensify its prevention-focused efforts in the coming years. Table 6 provides further details about the prevention-focused efforts highlighted in DOD's November 2014 report.

Table 6. Overview of Prevention-Focused Program Improvements Since 2013 Highlighted in DOD's November 2014 Report to the President

DOD's Prevention-Related Effort	Description
Updated the 2008 prevention strategy	In its report to the President, the Department of Defense (DOD) highlighted its efforts to update its 2008 prevention strategy, noting that while it had established a rationale for greater prevention activities and the means by which to promote prevention, it did not identify a means by which to promote unity of effort. As such, DOD undertook a variety of activities in 2013 to update its strategy that included a review of academic literature, visits to existing programs, and consultations with several subject-matter experts known for their innovative programs and research. In April 2014, using the consolidated results of its research and observations, DOD published the revised 2014-16 Sexual Assault Prevention Strategy. According to DOD, its updated strategy further enhances and augments existing efforts to prevent sexual assault by standardizing practices and programs across the department. DOD also notes that it researched promising practices and identified 10 elements that it plans to include in all sexual-assault prevention programs, including: (1) leadership involvement at all levels, (2) peer-to-peermentorship, (3) personal accountability, (4) resources, (5) community involvement, (6) deterrence, (7) communication, (8) incentives to promote prevention, (9) harm reduction, and (10) education and training.
RevisedWorkplace and Gender Relations Survey of Active Duty Members (WGRA) questions to more accurately calculate the prevalence of sexual assault in the military	Since 2006, DOD has been using the WGRA to identify the past-year prevalence of unwanted sexual contact, the survey term for a range of sexual crimes that include sexual assault in Sexual Assault Prevention and Response (SAPR) policy. The results of this survey have been used to determine, among other things, the progress of DOD's prevention efforts. Specifically, DOD uses the past-year prevalence of unwanted sexual contact to assess the extent of the problem and compares changes in prevalence over time in order to provide some indication of the effect of prevention work. In response to a request by the Senate Armed Services Committee for an independent review of the WGRA survey, DOD contracted with RAND in 2014 to conduct an independent assessment and, if necessary, to update the survey methodology and to administer the 2014 WGRA.

Table 6. (Continued)

DOD's Prevention-Related Effort	Description
	One notable change RAND made to the survey was to revise the question that had previously been used to measure the prevalence of "unwanted sexual contact" to now measure "sexual assault" and thus align with the terminology used and corresponding category of crimes specified in Article 120 of the Uniform Code of Military Justice.
DOD-wide standardization of SAPR core competencies and learning objectives	According to DOD, core competencies and learning objectives were identified, defined, and implemented in 2013 to help standardize SAPR training across the military. Specifically, DOD noted that specific SAPR monitoring, measures, and education were incorporated into normal command training, readiness, and safety forums, and that training was expanded to include Recruit Sustainment Programs. Further, DOD noted that SAPR training was enhanced and integrated into all levels of Professional Military Education, Pre-Command and Senior Enlisted Leader Training, Accession Training (within 14 days of going on active duty), Initial Military Training, SAPR Annual Training, and SAPR Pre- and Post-Deployment Training.
Command-climate assessment requirement and accountability for results	According to DOD, the Defense Equal Opportunity Management Institute (DEOMI) Organizational Climate Survey (DEOCS) is an assessment tool that commanders can use to solicit feedback from unit members on trends or behaviors within the unit. The survey also provides unit members with a way to confidentially communicate concerns, including those related to sexual assault. Responses to the survey are then used to spur additional information gathering and corrective action by unit leadership, as appropriate. In May 2013, DOD directed each of the military services to require commanders' yearly evaluations to include an assessment of their ability to promote climates of dignity and respect.[a]
Required at least annual command-climate surveys and additional oversight of results of the surveys	In July 2013, to help commanders better understand the factors at play within their units and within each command, the Secretary of Defense directed that they carry out—either annually or within 120 days of a change in unit command—the command-climate

DOD's Prevention-Related Effort	Description
	assessment process and that survey results be provided to both the unit commander and the next-level commander up in the chain of command.[b] According to DOD, this added another layer of oversight and provided another level of commander accountability as a part of a broader system of checks and balances. This was in response to Congress mandating that command-climate assessments regarding sexual assaults be conducted within 120 days of when a new commander assumes command and at least annually thereafter and that the results of these climate assessments be tracked and verified by the service Secretaries.[c]
Incorporated new and revised SAPR-related questions into command-climate surveys	According to DOD, command-climate surveys have been available to commanders for several years as a tool to assess unit climate. However, in January 2014, DOD updated its survey to include seven SAPR-related measures that are designed to assess (1) perceptions of safety, (2) chain-of-command support, (3) publicity of SAPR information, (4) unit reporting climate, (5) perceived barriers to reporting a sexual assault, (6) unit prevention climate, and (7) restricted reporting knowledge. The department is not collecting results of the survey's SAPR-related questions by individual commanders, but did note that it is consolidating results from across the services to help determine assessment methodologies of SAPR program effectiveness.
Developed a community of practice to disseminate promising prevention practices across DOD	In May 2014, the Secretary of Defense directed the Under Secretary of Defense for Personnel and Readiness to establish an implementation plan for a community of practice to share promising prevention practices and lessons learned. As a result, in 2014 DOD developed a community of practice, SAPR Connect, in order to leverage and advance research, as well as share promising practices and lessons learned with external experts, federal partners, military services, advocacy organizations, and educational institutions for prevention of sexual assault. SAPR Connect includes four interfaces: (1) virtual resources including video sharing and a social-media venue where members can post and share ideas; (2) face-to-face, in-person meetings; (3) quarterly webinars; (4) a community toolkit, such as SAPR-related policy and strategy documents, core competencies, and learning objectives for SAPR Training, and prevention-related posters, public service announcements, videos, and media materials.

Table 6. (Continued)

DOD's Prevention-Related Effort	Description
Created the Sexual Assault Prevention Innovation Award	In July 2014, DOD announced its Sexual Assault Prevention Innovation Award initiative. This initiative annually recognizes a group or individual (military or civilian) from each military component who contributed or developed an innovative idea, concept, methodology, or approach to positively affect sexual-assault prevention efforts either on an installation, in a deployed environment, or in a reserve component. A total of six awards were presented to individuals or groups from the military components in October 2014.
Emphasized prevention during its Sexual Assault Awareness Month	DOD placed an emphasis on prevention for its April 2015 Sexual Assault Awareness Month by changing its name from Sexual Assault Awareness Month to Sexual Assault Awareness and Prevention Month. Moreover, for its April 2015 Sexual Assault Awareness and Prevention Month, the 2015 theme was "Eliminate Sexual Assault. Know Your Part. Do Your Part," and it highlighted that everyone in the military has a role in prevention, no matter one's rank, position, or otherwise.
Augmented service academies'existing prevention programs to include the It's on Us campaign	In October 2014, the White House Task Force launched a new public awareness and education campaign known as, It's on Us. The *It's on Us* campaign is aimed at encouraging college students and all members of campus communities to be more engaged with campus sexual-assault prevention efforts. All three service academies have committed to participate in the It's on Us campaign and augment their existing prevention programs.

Source: GAO analysis of DOD data. | GAO-16-61

Note: Data are from DOD's November 2014 Report to the President of the United States on Sexual Assault Prevention and Response.

[a]Department of Defense, Secretary of Defense Memorandum, Enhancing Commander Accountability (Elevate Command Climate Surveys), (May 6, 2013).

[b]Department of Defense , Acting Under Secretary of Defense for Personnel and Readiness, Command Climate Assessments (July 25, 2013).

[c]Pub. L. No. 112-239, § 572, 126 Stat. 1753 (Jan. 2, 2013), as amended by Pub. L. No. 113-66, § 1721, 127 Stat. 970 (Dec. 26, 2013), codified at 10 U.S.C. § 1561 (note).

APPENDIX II: TIMELINE OF SELECTED GAO REPORTS AND DOD AND CONGRESSIONAL ACTIONS ON SEXUAL ASSAULT PREVENTION AND RESPONSE IN THE MILITARY

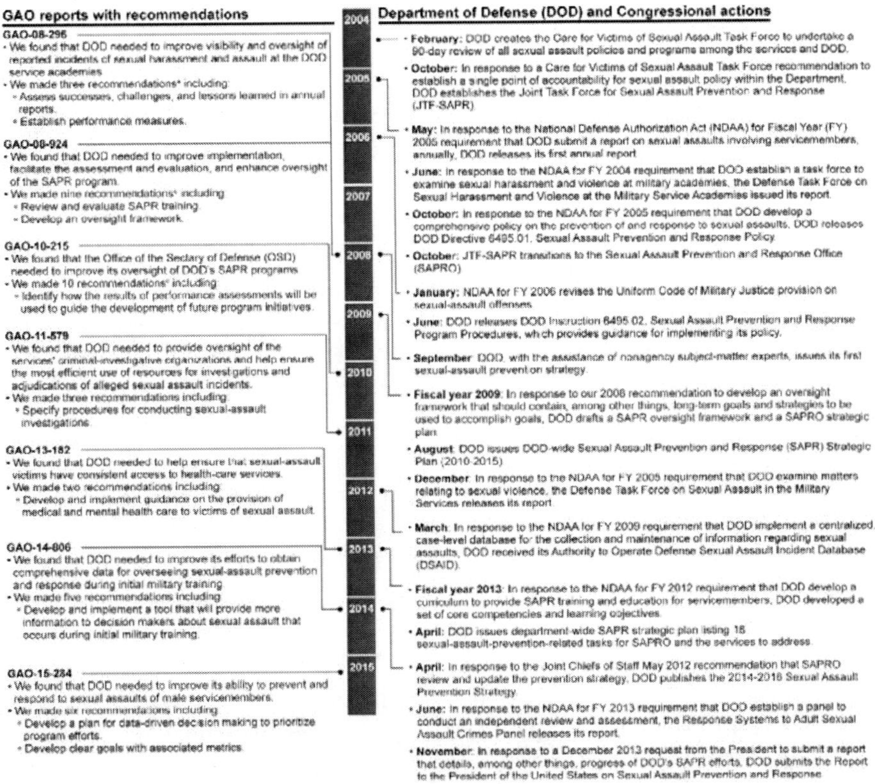

Source: GAO analysis of DOD documents and legislation. | GAO-16-61.

[a]We also made one recommendation related to the Coast Guard's efforts to prevent and respond to incidents of sexual assault.

[b]We also made two recommendations related to the Coast Guard's efforts to prevent and respond to incidents of sexual assault.

[c]We also made three recommendations related to the Coast Guard's efforts to prevent and respond to incidents of sexual assault.

Appendix III: Scope and Methodology

To determine the extent to which the Department of Defense (DOD) developed an effective strategy to prevent sexual assault in the military, we obtained and reviewed DOD's 2014-16 Sexual Assault Prevention Strategy. We also obtained and reviewed DOD's 2008 Sexual Assault Prevention Strategy, its 2012 Strategic Direction to the Joint Force on Sexual Assault Prevention and Response, its 2013 Sexual Assault Prevention and Response Strategic Plan, and relevant provisions in DOD and military service policies and guidance pertaining to the prevention of sexual assault incidents.[1] We interviewed officials in the Under Secretary of Defense for Personnel and Readiness's Sexual Assault Prevention and Response Office (SAPRO) as well as SAPR program officials with the Army, the Navy, the Marine Corps, and the Air Force to obtain an understanding of their respective roles in developing DOD's prevention strategy and the extent to which current military-service policies and guidance are consistent with the department's goals and objectives for preventing sexual assault.[2] We also interviewed officials from the Centers for Disease Control and Prevention (CDC) about their work developing and evaluating sexual-violence prevention programs and we reviewed and used CDC's social-ecological model and public-health model to evaluate the extent to which DOD identified elements such as domains, risk factors, and protective factors.[3] Further, we used CDC's program planning and development model to assess the extent to which DOD's 2014–16 prevention strategy and related documents contain all of the elements of a framework for effective sexual-violence prevention programs identified by CDC. We used Office of Management and Budget issued guidance on the budget preparation, submission, and execution, which, among other things, includes information regarding agency strategic reviews and mitigating risks related to achieving strategic objectives and performance goals.[4] We also used our prior work on effective agency strategic reviews, which has shown that it is important to review progress toward strategic objectives in that it can help to determine subsequent actions and that leaders and responsible managers should be held accountable for knowing the progress being made in achieving outcomes.[5] We compared DOD's strategy with prior related GAO reports to determine the extent to which the strategy addressed any of our previous recommendations on the prevention of sexual assault in the military.[6] We discussed the results of our analyses with officials in DOD SAPRO and officials in each of the military services responsible for developing and implementing DOD's strategy to prevent sexual assault in the military.

To determine the extent to which DOD implemented activities department-wide and at service-specific and joint installations related to the department's efforts to prevent sexual assault in the military, we reviewed DOD's 2008 and 2014-16 Sexual Assault Prevention Strategies, its 2012 Strategic Direction to the Joint Force on Sexual Assault Prevention and Response, its 2013 Sexual Assault Prevention and Response Strategic Plan, and relevant provisions in DOD and military service policies and guidance and the National Defense Authorization Acts for fiscal years 2004–2015 to identify any required prevention activities.[7] We also used CDC's evaluation model for public health programs to assess whether DOD's 2014-16 Sexual Assault Prevention Strategy included the six key elements of effective public health strategies identified by CDC.[8] To determine the extent to which the military services have implemented activities to prevent sexual assault, we visited three service-specific installations—Fort Shafter (Army), Schofield Barracks (Army), and Marine Corps Base Hawaii—and 1 joint base—Joint Base Pearl Harbor-Hickam (Navy and Air Force)—on Oahu, Hawaii. We chose these locations based on the reported high numbers of unrestricted reported sexual assaults relative to other installations within the same branch of military service and their close proximity to each other. During these visits, we met with military officials and program personnel who were identified as having a role in preventing sexual assault, including commanders, sexual-assault response coordinators, sexual harassment/assault response and prevention program managers, victim advocates, chaplains, criminal investigators, legal personnel, and medical and mental health-care providers to discuss their familiarity with DOD's prevention strategy and whether it had a role in the prevention activities sponsored at their respective installations.[9] We also discussed the extent of cross-service collaboration on sexual-assault prevention activities at these installations and compared them with guidance from the Joint Chiefs of Staff[10] and leading practices on interagency collaboration[11] to determine whether the military services have taken the steps necessary to effectively collaborate on similar prevention efforts.

To determine the extent to which DOD has developed performance measures to assess the effectiveness of its efforts to prevent sexual assault in the military, we reviewed DOD's 2013 Sexual Assault Prevention and Response Strategic Plan, its 2014 Report to the President of the United States on Sexual Assault Prevention and Response, its annual report on sexual assault in the military for fiscal year 2014, its 2014-16 Sexual Assault Prevention Strategy, and other related documents to identify performance measures that the department uses or plans to use to assess its progress in preventing sexual assault in the military.[12] Additionally, we met with DOD and military service officials to verify the performance measures identified and to discuss how they will be used to assess the effectiveness of the department's prevention efforts. We also compared DOD's five prevention-focused performance measures[13] with GAO criteria on key attributes of successful performance measures.[14]

We conducted this performance audit from August 2014 to October 2015 in accordance with generally accepted government auditing standards. Those standards require that we plan and perform the audit to obtain sufficient, appropriate evidence to provide a reasonable basis for our findings and conclusions based on our audit objectives. We believe that the evidence obtained provides a reasonable basis for our findings and conclusions based on our audit objectives.

RELATED GAO PRODUCTS

Military Personnel: Actions Needed to Address Sexual Assaults of Male Servicemembers. GAO-15-284. Washington, D.C.: March 19, 2015.

Military Personnel: DOD Needs to Take Further Actions to Prevent Sexual Assault during Initial Military Training. GAO-14-806. Washington, D.C.: September 9, 2014.

Military Personnel: DOD Has Taken Steps to Meet the Health Needs of Deployed Servicewomen, but Actions Are Needed to Enhance Care for Sexual Assault Victims. GAO-13-182. Washington, D.C.: January 29, 2013.

Military Personnel: Prior GAO Work on DOD's Actions to Prevent and Respond to Sexual Assault in the Military. GAO-12-571R. Washington, D.C.: March 30, 2012.

Preventing Sexual Harassment: DOD Needs Greater Leadership Commitment and an Oversight Framework. GAO-11-809. Washington, D.C.: September 21, 2011.

Military Justice: Oversight and Better Collaboration Needed for Sexual Assault Investigations and Adjudications. GAO-11-579. Washington, D.C.: June 22, 2011.

Military Personnel: DOD's and the Coast Guard's Sexual Assault Prevention and Response Programs Need to Be Further Strengthened. GAO-10-405T. Washington, D.C.: February 24, 2010.

Military Personnel: Additional Actions Are Needed to Strengthen DOD's and the Coast Guard's Sexual Assault Prevention and Response Programs. GAO-10-215. Washington, D.C.: February 3, 2010.

Military Personnel: Actions Needed to Strengthen Implementation and Oversight of DOD's and the Coast Guard's Sexual Assault Prevention and Response Programs. GAO-08-1146T. Washington, D.C.: September 10, 2008.

Military Personnel: DOD's and the Coast Guard's Sexual Assault Prevention and Response Programs Face Implementation and Oversight Challenges. GAO-08-924. Washington, D.C.: August 29, 2008.

Military Personnel: Preliminary Observations on DOD's and the Coast Guard's Sexual Assault Prevention and Response Programs. GAO-08-1013T. Washington, D.C.: July 31, 2008.

Military Personnel: The DOD and Coast Guard Academies Have Taken Steps to Address Incidents of Sexual Harassment and Assault, but Greater Federal Oversight Is Needed. GAO-08-296. Washington, D.C.: January 17, 2008.

End Notes

[1]Department of Defense, Department of Defense Annual Report on Sexual Assault in the Military, Fiscal Year 2014 (Apr. 29, 2015).

[2]RAND Corporation, Sexual Assault and Sexual Harassment in the U.S. Military: Volume 2. Estimates for Department of Defense Service Members from the 2014 RAND Military Workplace Study, Annex 1 to Department of Defense, Department of Defense Annual Report on Sexual Assault in the Military, Fiscal Year 2014. DOD typically conducts its Workplace and Gender Relations Surveys of active-duty servicemembers every 2 years to obtain the data used to calculate these estimates. In 2014, for similar purposes, RAND Corporation conducted the 2014 Military Workplace Study on behalf of DOD. The last three surveys were conducted for fiscal years 2010, 2012, and 2014. Prior to that, the last survey conducted was in 2006. For the purpose of our analysis, we only included reporting data and estimates of unwanted sexual contact or sexual assault back to 2008 since, according to Sexual Assault Prevention and Response Office (SAPRO) officials, data on reported sexual assaults prior to 2008 were not as reliable.

[3]See Ronald W. Reagan National Defense Authorization Act for Fiscal Year 2005, Pub. L. No. 108-375, § 577 (2004).

[4]GAO, Military Personnel: Actions Needed to Address Sexual Assaults of Male Servicemembers, GAO-15-284 (Washington, D.C.: Mar. 19, 2015).

[5]S. Rep. No. 113-176 at 115 (2014) accompanying S. 2410, a proposed bill for the National Defense Authorization Act for Fiscal Year 2015.

[6]See Centers for Disease Control and Prevention, Introduction to Program Evaluation for Public Health Programs: A Self-Study Guide (Atlanta, Ga.: October, 2011) and GAO, Managing for Results: Practices for Effective Agency Strategic Reviews, GAO-15-602 (Washington, D.C.: July 29, 2015).

[7]In its 2014-16 Sexual Assault Prevention Strategy, DOD uses the terms "initiatives" and "tasks" to refer to the activities it has identified will help to reduce sexual violence. For the purposes of this report, we refer to these initiatives and tasks as "activities."

[8]For more information about CDC's models and their use in evaluating public-health issues like reducing tobacco use see GAO, Program Evaluation: Strategies for Assessing How Information Dissemination Contributes to Agency Goals, GAO-02-923 (Washington, D.C.: Sept. 30, 2002).

[9]GAO-15-602. In that report, we analyzed and synthesized information gathered from a literature review, which covered public administration and public policy journals, business administration journals, our body of work on performance management and program evaluation, and other sources on policies and practices that can facilitate or challenge the effectiveness of strategic reviews as a decision-making tool. We also collected and analyzed documentation from six selected agencies' strategic-review processes and results, including guidance, meeting agendas, relevant evidence used to inform the review, and internal and published summaries of the results; conducted interviews with more than 30 performance-management and evaluation experts representing different levels of government, sectors (e.g., public; nonprofit; foundations), and nations, who had experience with implementing elements of strategic reviews or academic or consultative expertise in this area; and interviewed officials involved in conducting strategic reviews at six selected agencies and staff from the Office of Management and Budget and the Performance Improvement Council.

[10]The four military installations we visited were chosen based on the relatively high numbers of unrestricted reports of sexual assault relative to other installations within the same branch of service and on their close proximity to each other. While the information obtained at these four installations is not generalizable across DOD or any military service, it enabled us to obtain the perspectives of commanders and of officials who have responsibilities related to the prevention of sexual assault.

[11]We based the attributes on those that GAO identified in the following reports related to establishing successful performance measures. Specifically in GAO, Tax Administration: IRS Needs to Further Refine Its Tax Filing Season Performance Measures, GAO-03-143 (Washington, D.C.: Nov. 22, 2002), we identified linkage, measurable target, clarity, objectivity, reliability, limited overlap, core program activities, government-wide priorities, and balance as nine key attributes of successful performance measures using various sources, such as the Office of Management and Budget Circular No. A-11, Government Performance and Results Act of 1993, and prior GAO work. The prior GAO work includes GAO, Executive Guide: Effectively Implementing the Government Performance and Results Act, GAO/GGD-96-118 (Washington, D.C.: June 1996) and The Results Act: An Evaluator's Guide to Assessing Agency Annual Performance Plans, GAO/GGD-10.1.20 (Washington, D.C.: April 1998). In GAO, Defense Health Care Reform: Additional Implementation Details Would Increase Transparency of DOD's Plans and Enhance Accountability, GAO-14-49 (Washington, D.C.: Nov. 6, 2013), we identified baseline and trend data as an additional key attribute of successful performance measures by reviewing prior GAO work including GAO, Agency Performance Plans: Examples of Practices That Can Improve Usefulness to Decisionmakers, GAO/GGD/AIMD-99-69 (Washington, D.C.: Feb. 26, 1999).

[12]Department of Defense Directive 6495.01, Sexual Assault Prevention and Response (SAPR) Program (Jan. 23, 2012) (incorporating Change 2, Jan. 20, 2015). (Hereinafter cited as DOD Directive 6495.01).

[13]See the Ronald W. Reagan National Defense Authorization Act for Fiscal Year 2005, Pub. L. No. 108-375, § 577 (2004).

[14]DOD Directive 6495.01.

[15]DOD Directive 6495.01. DOD's annual reports to Congress on sexual assaults also cover cadets and midshipmen at the military service academies.

[16]In contrast to the other services, the Army's program that is responsible for dealing with sexual assaults also deals with sexual harassment. The Army's program is called the Sexual Harassment/Assault Response and Prevention (SHARP) program whereas the other programs are referred to as Sexual Assault Prevention and Response (SAPR). For purposes of consistency, we refer to SAPR programs for all services.

[17]Department of Defense Instruction 6495.02, Sexual Assault Prevention and Response (SAPR) Program Procedures (Mar. 28, 2013) (incorporating Change 2, July 7, 2015), encl. 5. (Hereinafter cited as DOD Instruction 6495.02.)

[18]See Army Regulation 600-20, Army Command Policy (Nov. 6, 2014); Air Force Instruction 90-6001, Sexual Assault Prevention and Response (SAPR) Program (May 21, 2015); Department of the Navy Instruction (SECNAVINST) 1752.4B, Sexual Assault Prevention and Response (Aug. 8, 2013); Department of the Navy, Marine Corps Order 1752.5B, Sexual Assault Prevention and Response (SAPR) Program (Mar. 1, 2013).

[19]Department of Defense, The Department of Defense Sexual Assault Prevention Strategy: Creating a National Benchmark Program (Sept. 30, 2008).

[20]DOD's 2008 strategy uses the spectrum-of-prevention model, which "describes several populations and levels of influence from the social ecology of an organization that are appropriate targets for intervention," as its framework. CDC uses the social ecological model, a similar framework based on the social ecology of an organization, for its guidance on effective sexual-violence prevention programs. See DOD, The Department of Defense Sexual Assault Prevention Strategy: Creating a National Benchmark Program; Centers for Disease Control and Prevention, Sexual Violence Prevention: Beginning the Dialogue (Atlanta, Ga.: 2004).

[21]Centers for Disease Control and Prevention, Introduction to Program Evaluation for Public Health Programs: A Self-Study Guide (Atlanta, Ga.: October 2011).

[22]Department of Defense, Strategic Management Plan: The Business of Defense FY2014- 2015, July 1, 2013.

[23]GAO-15-602.

[24]CDC, Sexual Violence Prevention: Beginning the Dialogue.

[25]Office of Management and Budget, Circular No. A-11: Preparation, Submission, and Execution of the Budget, at § 270.24 (June 2015).

[26]The 2014 RAND Military Workplace Study is an independent assessment of past-year sexual assault prevalence in DOD. RAND Corporation, Sexual Assault and Sexual Harassment in the U.S. Military: Volume 2. Estimates for Department of Defense Service Members from the 2014 Rand Military Workplace Study.

[27]In addition to DOD SAPRO and the military departments and services, DOD's 2014–16 Sexual Assault Prevention Strategy identifies the National Guard Bureau as an office with primary responsibility for implementing certain activities. However, the National Guard Bureau was not included in the scope of this report. S. 1376, a bill for the National Defense Authorization Act for Fiscal year 2016, includes a provision for GAO to report on the extent to which the Army National Guard and the Army Reserve have developed policies and procedures to, among other things, prevent and respond to sexual assault.

[28]Department of the Navy, Headquarters United States Marine Corps, Sexual Assault Prevention and Response (SAPR) – Advance and Sustain Appropriate Culture (Oct. 9, 2014).

[29]See Army Regulation 600-20, Army Command Policy; Air Force Instruction 90-6001, Sexual Assault Prevention and Response (SAPR) Program; Department of the Navy Instruction

(SECNAVINST) 1752.4B, Sexual Assault Prevention and Response; Department of the Navy, Marine Corps Order 1752.5B, Sexual Assault Prevention and Response (SAPR) Program.

[30]Joint Chiefs of Staff, Strategic Direction to the Joint Force on Sexual Assault Prevention and Response (May 7, 2012).

[31]Department of Defense Directive 1350.2, Department of Defense Military Equal Opportunity Program (Aug. 18, 1995) (incorporating Change 2, June 8, 2015), defines sexual harassment as a form of sex discrimination that involves unwelcome sexual advances, requests for sexual favors, and other verbal or physical conduct of a sexual nature when submission to such conduct is made either explicitly or implicitly a term or condition of a person's job, pay, or career; or submission to or rejection of such conduct by a person is used as a basis for career or employment decisions affecting that person; or such conduct has the purpose or effect of unreasonably interfering with an individual's work performance or creates an intimidating, hostile, or offensive working environment.

[32]DOD, Directive 6495.01, Sexual Assault Prevention and Response (SAPR) Program, was issued on October 6, 2005. The current directive, which was reissued on January 23, 2012, also requires the Under Secretary of Defense for Personnel and Readiness to develop metrics to measure compliance and effectiveness of SAPR training, awareness, prevention, and response policies and programs.

[33]We also made additional recommendations to DOD and the Coast Guard. DOD and the Coast Guard concurred with our recommendations. See GAO, Military Personnel: DOD's and the Coast Guard's Sexual Assault Prevention and Response Programs Face Implementation and Oversight Challenges, GAO-08-924 (Washington, D.C.: Aug. 29, 2008).

[34]See National Defense Authorization Act for Fiscal Year 2010, Pub. L. No. 111-84, § 567 (2009).

[35]DOD identified 12 metrics and 6 nonmetrics in its November 2014 report the President. DOD defined its "non-metrics" as items that address the military justice process, and stated that there will be no effort to direct the aspects or outcomes of these nonmetrics, as doing so may constitute unlawful command influence on military justice. The six nonmetrics are not linked to DOD's prevention line of effort. Throughout this report, we will refer to DOD's 12 metrics as performance measures.

[36]Department of Defense, "Provisional Metrics on Sexual Assault," app. B to DOD, Department of Defense, Report to the President of the United States on Sexual Assault Prevention and Response (Nov. 25, 2014). In April 2015, DOD finalized and republished its set of metrics in the Department of Defense Annual Report on Sexual Assault in the Military, Fiscal Year 2014, Appendix B: Metrics on Sexual Assault.

[37]SAPRO identified five lines of effort—prevention, investigation, accountability, advocacy/victim assistance, and assessment. All but the assessment line of effort are linked to 1 or more of the 12 performance measures. The purpose of the assessment line of effort is to identify qualitative and quantitative measures to inform programs and policies. For this report, we analyzed DOD's 5 measures linked to DOD's prevention line of effort. Measures linked to investigation, accountability, and advocacy/victim assistance were not included in our analysis because these measures are outside the scope of this review.

[38]We based these 10 attributes on those that GAO identified in the following reports related to establishing successful performance measures. Specifically in GAO-03-143, we identified linkage, measurable target, clarity, objectivity, reliability, limited overlap, core program activities, government-wide priorities, and balance as nine key attributes of successful

performance measures using various sources, such as the Office of Management and Budget Circular No. A-11, Government Performance and Results Act of 1993, and prior GAO work. The prior GAO work includes GAO/GGD-96-118 and GAO/GGD-10.1.20. In GAO, Defense Health Care Reform: Additional Implementation Details Would Increase Transparency of DOD's Plans and Enhance Accountability, GAO-14-49 (Washington, D.C.: Nov. 6, 2013), we identified baseline and trend data as an additional key attribute of successful performance measures by reviewing prior GAO work including GAO, Agency Performance Plans: Examples of Practices That Can Improve Usefulness to Decisionmakers, GAO/GGD/AIMD-99-69 (Washington, D.C.: Feb. 26, 1999).

[39]Some earlier work includes GAO/GGD-96-118 and GAO/GGD-10.1.20.

[40]The four characteristics are overarching, thus there is not necessarily a direct link between any one attribute and any one characteristic.

[41]See GAO-03-143, GAO/GGD-96-118, GAO/GGD-10.1.20, and GAO-14-49.

[42]We have recently reported on an agency program where not enough research existed to determine performance measures or outcomes. For example, National Aeronautics and Space Administration officials told us that because it can be difficult to measure progress towards long-term, scientific discovery-oriented outcomes, they rely on underlying multiyear performance goals, annual performance indicators, and milestones to better plan for and understand progress towards objectives. See GAO-15-602.

[43]GAO-15-284.

[44] A convenience sample is a nonprobability sample, from which inferences cannot be made. Convenience sampling involves selecting the sample from the part of the population that is convenient to reach.

End Notes for Appendix III

[1]Department of Defense, 2014-16 Sexual Assault Prevention Strategy (Apr. 30, 2014); Department of Defense, Sexual Assault Prevention and Response Strategic Plan (Apr. 30, 2013); Joint Chiefs of Staff, Strategic Direction to the Joint Force on Sexual Assault Prevention and Response (May 7, 2012); Department of Defense, The Department of Defense Sexual Assault Prevention Strategy: Creating a National Benchmark Program (Sept. 30, 2008).

[2]In contrast to the other services, the Army's program that is responsible for dealing with sexual assaults also deals with sexual harassment. The Army's program is called the Sexual Harassment/Assault Response and Prevention (SHARP) program whereas the other programs are referred to as Sexual Assault Prevention and Response (SAPR).

[3]Centers for Disease Control and Prevention, Sexual Violence Prevention: Beginning the Dialogue (Atlanta, Ga.: 2004). For more information about CDC's models and their use in evaluating public-health issues like reducing tobacco use, see GAO, Program Evaluation: Strategies for Assessing How Information Dissemination Contributes to Agency Goals, GAO-02-923 (Washington, D.C.: Sept. 30, 2002).

[4]Office of Management and Budget, Circular No. A-11: Preparation, Submission, and Execution of the Budget, at § 270.24 (June 2015).

[5]GAO, Managing for Results: Practices for Effective Agency Strategic Reviews, GAO-15-602 (Washington, D.C.: July 29, 2015). In that report, GAO analyzed and synthesized information gathered from a literature review, which covered public administration and

public-policy journals, business-administration journals, GAO's body of work on performance management and program evaluation, and other sources on policies and practices that can facilitate or challenge the effectiveness of strategic reviews as a decision-making tool. GAO also collected and analyzed documentation from six selected agencies' strategic-review processes and results, including guidance, meeting agendas, relevant evidence used to inform the review, and internal and published summaries of the results; conducted interviews with more than 30 performance-management and evaluation experts representing different levels of government, sectors (e.g., public; nonprofit; foundations), and nations, who had experience with implementing elements of strategic reviews or academic or consultative expertise in this area; and interviewed officials involved in conducting strategic reviews at six selected agencies, and staff from the Office of Management and Budget and the Performance Improvement Council.

[6]GAO, Military Personnel: The DOD and Coast Guard Academies Have Taken Steps to Address Incidents of Sexual Harassment and Assault, but Greater Federal Oversight Is Needed, GAO-08-296 (Washington, D.C.: Jan. 17, 2008); Military Personnel: DOD's and the Coast Guard's Sexual Assault Prevention and Response Programs Face Implementation and Oversight Challenges, GAO-08-924 (Washington, D.C.: Aug. 29, 2008); Military Personnel: Additional Actions Are Needed to Strengthen DOD's and the Coast Guard's Sexual Assault Prevention and Response Programs, GAO-10-215 (Washington, D.C.: Feb. 3, 2010); Military Justice: Oversight and Better Collaboration Needed for Sexual Assault Investigations and Adjudications, GAO-11-579 (Washington, D.C.: June 22, 2011); Military Personnel: DOD Has Taken Steps to Meet the Health Needs of Deployed Servicewomen, but Actions Are Needed to Enhance Care for Sexual Assault Victims, GAO-13-182 (Washington, D.C.: Jan. 29, 2013); Military Personnel: DOD Needs to Take Further Actions to Prevent Sexual Assault during Initial Military Training, GAO-14-806 (Washington, D.C.: Sept. 9, 2014); Military Personnel: Actions Needed to Address Sexual Assaults of Male Servicemembers, GAO-15-284 (Washington, D.C.: Mar. 19, 2015).

[7]Department of Defense Directive 6495.01, Sexual Assault Prevention and Response (SAPR) Program (Jan. 23, 2012) (incorporating Change 2, effective Jan. 20, 2015); Department of Defense Instruction 6495.02, Sexual Assault Prevention and Response (SAPR) Program Procedures (Mar. 28, 2013) (incorporating Change 2, July 7, 2015); Department of the Navy, SECNAV Instruction 1752.4B, Sexual Assault Prevention and Response (Aug. 8, 2013); Department of the Navy, Marine Corps Order 1752.5B, Sexual Assault Prevention and Response (SAPR) Program, (Mar. 1, 2013); Department of the Air Force, Air Force Instruction 90-6001, Sexual Assault Prevention and Response (SAPR) Program (May 21, 2015); Department of the Army, Army Regulation 600-20, Army Command Policy, Chapter 8: Sexual Assault Prevention and Response Program (Nov. 6, 2014).

[8]Centers for Disease Control and Prevention, Introduction to Program Evaluation for Public Health Programs: A Self-Study Guide (Atlanta, Ga.: October, 2011).

[9]While the information obtained at these installations is not generalizable across DOD or any military service, it enabled us to obtain the perspectives of commanders and of officials who have responsibilities related to the prevention of sexual assault.

[10]Joint Chiefs of Staff, Strategic Direction to the Joint Force on Sexual Assault Prevention and Response (May 7, 2012).

[11]GAO, Managing for Results: Key Considerations for Implementing Interagency Collaborative Mechanisms, GAO-12-1022 (Washington, D.C.: Sept. 27, 2012).

[12]Department of Defense, Report to the President of the United States on Sexual Assault Prevention and Response (Nov. 25, 2014); Department of Defense, Department of Defense Annual Report on Sexual Assault in the Military, Fiscal Year 2014 (Apr. 29, 2015).

[13]DOD included 12 metrics and 6 nonmetrics in its 2014 report to the President and 2014 annual report on sexual assault. Five of the 12 metrics were designed to specifically measure the effectiveness of its prevention efforts.

[14]We reviewed the following GAO reports related to establishing successful performance measures: (1) GAO, Tax Administration: IRS Needs to Further Refine Its Tax Filing Season Performance Measures, GAO-03-143 (Washington, D.C.: Nov. 22, 2002). For that report, GAO identified nine key attributes of successful performance measures using various sources, such as the Office of Management and Budget Circular No. A-11, the Government Performance and Results Act of 1993, and prior GAO work. The prior GAO work includes GAO, Executive Guide: Effectively Implementing the Government Performance and Results Act, GAO/GGD-96-118 (Washington, D.C.: June 1996) and The Results Act: An Evaluator's Guide to Assessing Agency Annual Performance Plans, GAO/GGD-10.1.20 (Washington, D.C.: April 1998); (2) GAO, Defense Health Care Reform: Additional Implementation Details Would Increase Transparency of DOD's Plans and Enhance Accountability, GAO-14-49 (Washington, D.C.: Nov. 6, 2013). For that report, GAO identified an additional key attribute of successful performance measures by reviewing prior GAO work including GAO, Agency Performance Plans: Examples of Practices That Can Improve Usefulness to Decisionmakers, GAO/GGD/AIMD-99-69 (Washington, D.C.: Feb. 26, 1999).

In: Sexual Assault Prevention …
Editor: Jonathan Maldonado

ISBN: 978-1-63485-351-4

Chapter 3

DEPARTMENT OF DEFENSE ANNUAL REPORT ON SEXUAL ASSAULT IN THE MILITARY, FISCAL YEAR 2014*

Department of Defense

UNDER SECRETARY OF DEFENSE
4000 DEFENSE PENTAGON
WASHINGTON, D.C. 20301-4000

The Honorable John McCain
Chairman
Committee on Armed Services
United States Senate
Washington, DC 20510
April 29 2015

Dear Mr. Chairman:

Section 1631 of the Ike Skelton National Defense Authorization Act (NDAA) for Fiscal Year (FY) 2011 requires the Secretary of Defense to submit to the Committees on Armed Services of the Senate and House of

---

* This is an edited, reformatted and augmented version of a report issued to Congress, May 1, 2015.

Representatives an annual report on the sexual assaults involving members of the Armed Forces during the preceding year, including reports from each of the Military Departments.

The enclosed "Department of Defense Fiscal Year 2014 Annual Report on Sexual Assault in the Military" presents statistics and analysis of reports of sexual assault during FY 2014 and discusses policy and program improvements to the Sexual Assault Prevention and Response (SAPR) program of the Department of Defense (DoD). The numerical data and statistics contained in this report are drawn from metrics identified in the Department's evaluation plan, which fulfills additional reporting requirements outlined in the NDAAs for FY 2011, 2012, and 2013.

This report documents considerable progress to address sexual assault in the military. While there are positive indicators, more must be done to eliminate the crimes that constitute sexual assault and implement enduring culture change. In FY 2015, the DoD will continue to work together with the Services to incorporate best practices and reforms that improve our ability to address the crime.

Thank you for your commitment to our Service members. I am sending a similar letter, with the Department's report, to the Chairman of the House Committee on Armed Services.

Sincerely,
Brad Carson
Acting

Enclosures: As stated

cc:
The Honorable Jack Reed
Ranking Member

* * *

UNDER SECRETARY OF DEFENSE
4000 DEFENSE PENTAGON
WASHINGTON, D.C. 20301-4000

The Honorable Mac Thornberry
Chairman

Committee on Armed Services
U.S. House of Representatives
Washington, DC 20515
April 29 2015

Dear Mr. Chairman:

Section 1631 of the Ike Skelton National Defense Authorization Act (NDAA) for Fiscal Year (FY) 2011 requires the Secretary of Defense to submit to the Committees on Armed Services of the Senate and House of Representatives an annual report on the sexual assaults involving members of the Armed Forces during the preceding year, including reports from each of the Military Departments.

The enclosed "Department of Defense Fiscal Year 2014 Annual Report on Sexual Assault in the Military" presents statistics and analysis of reports of sexual assault during FY 2014 and discusses policy and program improvements to the Sexual Assault Prevention and Response (SAPR) program of the Department of Defense (DoD). The numerical data and statistics contained in this report are drawn from metrics identified in the Department's evaluation plan, which fulfills additional reporting requirements outlined in the NDAAs for FY 2011, 2012, and 2013.

This report documents considerable progress to address sexual assault in the military. While there are positive indicators, more must be done to eliminate the crimes that constitute sexual assault and implement enduring culture change. In FY 2015, the DoD will continue to work together with the Services to incorporate best practices and reforms that improve our ability to address the crime.

Thank you for your commitment to our Service members. I am sending a similar letter, with the Department's report, to the Chairman of the Senate Committee on Armed Services.

Sincerely,
Brad Carson
Acting
Enclosures: As stated

cc:
The Honorable Adam Smith
Ranking Member

EXECUTIVE SUMMARY

Sexual assault is a crime that has no place in the United States Armed Forces.[1] The Department of Defense worked aggressively during fiscal year 2014 to sustain and enhance its prevention and response system, through both programmatic initiatives and policy changes to combat sexual assault. The Department of Defense has many options in place to help victims[2] recover, address their safety, document the alleged crime, and understand their legal options.

Federal law requires the Department to provide Congress with an annual report on sexual assaults involving members of the Armed Forces. This report satisfies the requirement, which is in section 1631 of the Ike Skelton National Defense Authorization Act for Fiscal Year 2011 (Public Law 111-383).[3,4] The report presents the Department's programmatic activities and policy enhancements and also provides an analysis of reports of sexual assault made during fiscal year 2014 (October 1, 2013 through September 30, 2014). Included with this report are supplementary reports from the Secretaries of the Military Departments, the Chief of the National Guard Bureau, and a report submitted by RAND Corporation for the *2014 RAND Military Workplace Study*.[5]

Report to the President of the United States on Sexual Assault Prevention and Response

In December 2013, the President of the United States directed the Secretary of Defense to provide a report on the Department's progress in addressing the issue of sexual assault, to include a review of the military justice system, by December 2014. As delivered to the White House on December 4, 2014, and shared with Congress, the *Report to the President of the United States on Sexual Assault Prevention and Response* encompassed the key programmatic initiatives and policy enhancements undertaken by the Department in fiscal years 2012 through 2014, with accompanying rationale, as well as synopses and evidence of progress.

The report also contained information from the new *Survivor Experience Survey*[6] and a military focus group effort on sexual assault prevention and response, both fielded by the Defense Manpower Data Center; top-line results of the *RAND Military Workplace Study;* and provisional statistical data on the Department's fiscal year 2014 reports of sexual assault. Provisional metrics and non-metrics developed by the Department, and approved by the White House, were also provided to assess strengths and opportunities for improvement in the Department's sexual assault prevention and response program. In order to avoid duplication of effort and reporting, this report – the *Fiscal Year 2014 Annual Report on Sexual Assault in the Military* – is intended to provide Congress with an update to the information included in the *Report to the President*, as well as other information required by law.

Data Validation Efforts for Fiscal Year 2014 Annual Report

In the *Report to the President*, the Department provided provisional statistical data on sexual assault for fiscal year 2014. These data were deemed provisional because there was insufficient time to thoroughly and completely collect and validate the thousands of reports and case dispositions received in fiscal year 2014.

In this report, the Department provides final statistical data. Comprehensive data validation efforts by the Department, in the intervening time between the two reports account for small differences between the provisional statistical data and the final data presented here.

Fiscal Year 2014 Data Findings

From fiscal year 2012 to fiscal year 2013, there was an unprecedented 53% increase in victim reports of sexual assault. In fiscal year 2014, the high level of reporting seen in fiscal year 2013 was sustained with 6,131 reports[7] of sexual assault[8] (see Figure 1, below). This figure represents an increase of 11% over fiscal year 2013 numbers. In fiscal year 2014, victims made 4,660 Unrestricted Reports[9] and 1,840 initial Restricted Reports[10] of sexual assault. At the close of fiscal year 2014, 1,471 reports remained Restricted. Over time, the percentage of victims who convert their Restricted Reports to Unrestricted Reports has remained relatively stable with an average of 15%. However, in fiscal year 2014, the conversion rate increased to 20%.

Overall, surveys of sexual assault victims suggest that those who reported their sexual assault were satisfied with their decision. According to the *2014 RAND Military Workplace Study*, approximately 72% of Service member victims who indicated that they reported their sexual assault said they would make the same decision if they had to do it over again. Furthermore, according to the *Survivor Experience Survey*, 73% of Service member victims who participated in the survey indicated that, based on their overall experience of reporting, they would recommend that others report.

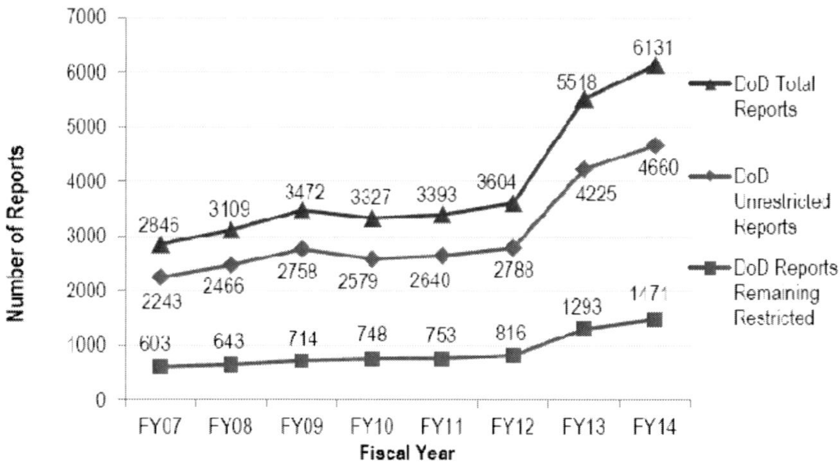

Figure 1. Reports of Sexual Assault to DoD, FY 2007 - FY 2014.

According to the *2014 RAND Military Workplace Study,* the percentage of active duty women who experienced unwanted sexual contact in the past year declined from an estimated 6.1% in 2012 to an estimated 4.3% in 2014, a statistically significant decrease.[11] For active duty men, the estimated prevalence rate of unwanted sexual contact trended downwards from 1.2% in 2012 to 0.9% in 2014.[12, 13, 14] Based on these prevalence rates, an estimated 18,900 Service members experienced unwanted sexual contact in 2014, down from the 26,000 Service member victims estimated in 2012.[15]

Assessment of Progress

Out of the 6,131 reports of sexual assault in FY 2014, there were 4,768 Service Member *victims* who made a report for an incident that occurred during military Service[16], a 16% increase from FY 2013. As reflected in Figure 2, 25%, or about 1 in 4 of the estimated 18,900 Service member victims who experienced unwanted sexual contact made a Restricted or Unrestricted Report for an incident that occurred during military service. In fiscal year 2012, 11%, or about 1 in 10 of the estimated Service members who experienced the crime reported it. The estimated 25% reporting rate in fiscal year 2014 is the highest ever recorded for the Military Services. In other words, in fiscal year 2014, the estimated gap between reporting and prevalence among Service members decreased to its narrowest point since the Department began tracking these data. When Service members who experienced sexual assault come forward to make a report, the Department can provide victims with support and hold offenders appropriately accountable.

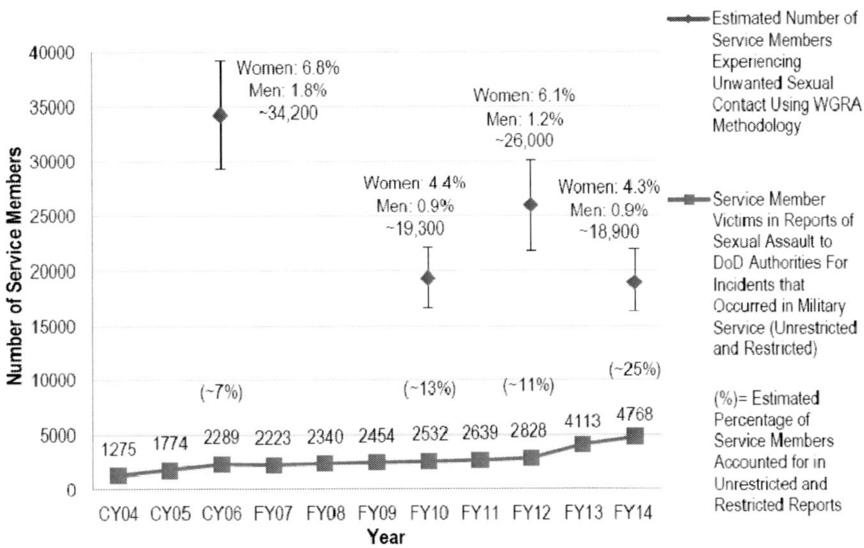

Figure 2. Estimated Number of Service Members Experiencing Unwanted Sexual Contact Based on Past-Year Prevalence Rates versus Number of Service Member Victims in Reports of Sexual Assault for Incidents Occurring During Military Service, CY 2004 – FY 2014.[17]

Efforts to Assess and Address Retaliation

Following the President's request in 2013 for a report on sexual assault, the Department selected a number of metrics to measure progress in sexual assault prevention and response, including a metric to assess "perceived retaliation."[18] Historically, the Department has asked about retaliation on surveys to better assess victim well-being and to understand the stressors victims experience following a report of sexual assault. The Department of Defense collects this information in order to better adjust support programs and tailor services and training to match victims' needs. The White House-approved metric will enhance the Department's ability to measure progress in this area.

In order to gain a more comprehensive understanding of retaliation perceived by victims, the Department sought multiple sources of data:

- Command Climate Perspective (Defense Equal Opportunity Management Institute Organizational Climate Survey)
  - The Defense Equal Opportunity Management Institute Organizational Climate Survey included six items to assess command climate indicators of retaliation against victims who choose to report sexual assault. Overall, Service members who completed the Defense Equal Opportunity Management Institute Organizational Climate Survey in 2014 perceived the potential for retaliation from their command and unit members to be low (i.e., they perceived a favorable climate associated with reporting).
- The 2014 RAND Military Workplace Study
  - Of the 4.3% of women who indicated experiencing unwanted sexual contact in the past year and who reported the matter to a military authority or organization, 62% perceived some form of professional or social retaliation, administrative action, and/or punishment associated with their report (53% social retaliation, 35% adverse administrative action, 32% professional retaliation, and 11% punishment for infraction[19]). However, because the data do not provide for the circumstances regarding administrative action or actions, which victims perceive as professional retaliation, we are unable to draw any conclusions regarding these numbers. Data for men were not reportable due to the small number of male respondents in this category.
- The 2014 Survivor Experience Survey
  - In the Survivor Experience Survey, a similar pattern was observed concerning retaliation, with 59% of respondents perceiving social retaliation and 40% of respondents perceiving professional retaliation.

In order to better assess the experience of retaliation and identify potential points for intervention, the Department plans to conduct a systematic review of retaliation allegations made to the Service commands and Inspectors General. In addition, the Department will revise its survey questions to better align with Department policy and law addressing reprisal and ostracism. Finally, the Department will follow up on installation case management group execution of inquiring about allegations of retaliation during monthly meetings.[20] These attempts to better define the scope of the problem and capture the efforts taken to address this unacceptable behavior will inform Department-wide efforts to prevent retaliation associated with reporting sexual assault.

NDAA Requirement Implementation

The last three National Defense Authorization Acts focused significantly on sexual assault prevention and response issues with 71 sections of law containing more than 100 unique requirements, to include 16 congressional reporting requirements. The National Defense Authorization Act for Fiscal Year 2014 includes 33 sections of law, representing more than 50 individual provisions within those 33 National Defense Authorization Act sections. It contains the most sweeping reform to the Uniform Code of Military Justice since 1968, with 16 military justice provisions.

Implementation of the fiscal year 2014 provisions is ongoing, and many have already been implemented. The issuance of policy documents, including Change 2 to the Sexual Assault Prevention and Response Instruction, updates to Military Personnel Policy,[21] and revisions of two Inspector General policy documents,[22] incorporate the remaining provisions.

Programmatic and Policy Updates Implemented in Fiscal Year 2014

From fiscal year 2012 to fiscal year 2014, the Secretary of Defense directed 41 initiatives that fundamentally reformed how the military prevents, responds to, and adjudicates sexual assault.[23] Throughout the year, the Department worked diligently to comply with these initiatives. By the end of the fiscal year, 6 initiatives remained in progress. Many of the Secretary of Defense initiatives have been codified in National Defense Authorization Acts.

The Department of Defense Sexual Assault Prevention and Response Office organizes and reports the Department's progress in the sexual assault prevention and response program using the five lines of effort from the *Department of Defense Sexual Assault Prevention and Response Strategic Plan*, revised and published in April 2013 and updated in January 2015. The five lines of effort are aligned across the Military Services and the National Guard Bureau, providing a coordinated approach to sexual assault prevention and response. During fiscal year 2014, the Department implemented several programmatic and policy enhancements to meet the objectives of the lines of effort:

- Prevention: In fiscal year 2014, the Department continued its focus on prevention through the *2014-2016 Department of Defense Sexual*

Assault Prevention Strategy. The new strategy provides a roadmap for the delivery of consistent and effective prevention initiatives through empirically based promising practices. It considers the complex interplay between individual, relationship, community, and societal factors and allows the Department to address those factors that put people at risk for experiencing or perpetrating violence. While there is no single "silver bullet" solution, this innovative prevention strategy allows for new promising practices to be incorporated, assessed, and adapted accordingly.

- Investigation: The objective of the Investigation Line of Effort is to achieve high competence in the investigation of sexual assault. In order to reach this objective, the Department established the Special Victim Investigation and Prosecution Capability, which became fully operational in January 2014. This initiative is not a specific person or team but a capability available globally throughout the Department to investigate and prosecute adult sexual assault offenses. The personnel who are part of the capability receive specialized training for their roles, which enhances the Department's ability to produce timely and accurate investigative results.
- Accountability: Holding offenders[24] appropriately accountable is the objective of the Accountability Line of Effort, and victim participation in the military justice process is key to holding offenders appropriately accountable. As a means to provide advice and advocacy, as well as empower victims to participate in the justice system, in addition to the specialized prosecution capability noted above in the Special Victim Investigation and Prosecution Capability, the Military Departments established the Special Victims' Counsel/Victims' Legal Counsel Program, which reached full operating capability in January 2014. These programs provide victims with military judge advocates who provide independent, personalized legal advice and representation to victims of sexual assault, protecting their rights and empowering them to successfully navigate the military justice system.
- Advocacy/Victim Assistance: Throughout fiscal year 2014, Department efforts also focused on the delivery of consistent and effective victim support, response, and reporting options. The Department implemented provisions to expand victims' rights by giving them the opportunity to provide input during the post-trial action phase. The Department also took steps to enhance screening

criteria for personnel working with victims and issued guidance regarding document retention for 50 years regardless of the type of the report. All of these efforts demonstrate the Department's continued commitment of providing victims with a dynamic sexual assault prevention and response system.

- Assessment: In fiscal year 2014, the Department of Defense took steps to effectively standardize, measure, analyze, assess, and report program progress. The Defense Manpower Data Center fielded, across all Department components, the first ever *Survivor Experience Survey*, which also provided data included in the *Report to the President*. The purposes of the *Survivor Experience Survey* were to capture feedback on victim satisfaction with the response system, assess the impact of recent initiatives and policies on victims, and meet the *Report to the President* requirement. The feedback from the *2014 Survivor Experience Survey* allows the Department to analyze its program and make more informed decisions on future initiatives.

Way Forward

This report shows that, in fiscal year 2014, the estimated prevalence of sexual assault decreased across the Department and that the estimated proportion of victims choosing to report the crime has increased to an unprecedented level. Despite these positive indicators, the Department of Defense's commitment to progress is enduring and includes ongoing work with the Services to incorporate best practices and reforms that improve its ability to address the crime. Every Service member must participate in creating a culture where sexist behaviors, sexual harassment, and sexual assault are not tolerated, condoned, or ignored. Leaders will be held accountable for establishing the appropriate command climate. The Department's success relies on the full participation of every Service member and leader in implementing this culture change.

The Department of Defense continues to implement the Response Systems to Adult Sexual Assault Crimes Panel recommendations, Secretary of Defense initiatives, and National Defense Authorization Act requirements. Furthermore, the Secretary of Defense issued additional initiatives today. The Secretaries of the Military Departments, in collaboration with the Acting Under Secretary of Defense for Personnel and Readiness, will incorporate insights derived from the *2014 RAND Military Workplace Study* into prevention training for sexual harassment, sexual assault, and reporting-related retaliation. Additionally, the Acting Under Secretary of Defense for Personnel and Readiness will assess clinical interventions that address the specific needs of men and women who are seeking treatment for sexual assault. The Acting Under Secretary of Defense for Personnel and Readiness will also conduct force-wide sexual assault and sexual harassment prevalence surveys biennially for the Military Services and National Guard, using the measures created for the *2014 RAND Military Workplace Study*, consistent with title 10 United States Code section 481. In alternate years, force-wide focus groups will be conducted by the Defense Manpower Data Center to obtain feedback from the field. To better respect Service member survey burden and privacy, all other entities within the Department of Defense will refrain from conducting force-wide surveys for determining the prevalence of sexual assault and sexual harassment. The surveys and focus groups will be developed and conducted in collaboration with the Secretaries of the Military Departments, the Chiefs of the Military Services, and the National Guard Bureau. Finally, the Acting Under Secretary of Defense for Personnel and Readiness, in collaboration with the Secretaries of the Military Departments and the Department of Defense Inspector General, will establish a comprehensive strategy to prevent retaliation against Service members who report or intervene on behalf of the victim in instances of sexual assault and other crimes.

INTRODUCTION

Report Requirement

This report is the Department of Defense (*DoD) Fiscal Year (FY) 2014 Annual Report on Sexual Assault in the Military*.[25] This is the Department's 11th Annual Report on sexual assault covering sexual assault reports made during FY 2014 (October 1, 2013 through September 30, 2014).[26] This report also describes many of the Department's sexual assault prevention programs, initiatives, and policy enhancements developed and implemented during FY 2014. The report organizes and communicates the Department's progress using the five lines of effort (LOE) from the *DoD Sexual Assault Prevention and Response (SAPR) Strategic Plan*, which was revised in FY 2015.

Report to the President of the United States on Sexual Assault Prevention and Response

On December 20, 2013, President Barack Obama directed the Department to provide a comprehensive report detailing major improvements in DoD's SAPR programs, including reforms to the military justice system.

In December 2014, the Secretary of Defense provided the President with the requested report, illustrating the substantial progress made by the Department in the preceding three years. The full DoD report, *Report to the President of the United States on Sexual Assault Prevention and Response*, was also shared with Congress and can be found at http://www.sapr.mil/index.php/annual-reports. In addition, each of the Military Departments, the National Guard Bureau (NGB), and the United States Coast Guard (USCG) provided supplemental reports detailing their respective progress. The DoD Office of General Counsel (OGC) also provided a synopsis of the recent reforms to the military justice system. The executive summary from the President's report is enclosed at Annex 2 of this report.

The *Report to the President* also contained:

- Provisional data and analyses of sexual assault reports made in FY 2014;
- Top-line results from the *2014 RAND Military Workplace Study (RMWS)*;
- Results from the new *2014 Survivor Experience Survey (SES)* fielded by the Defense Manpower Data Center (DMDC); and
- Results from the Service member focus group effort also fielded by the DMDC.

In order to avoid duplication of effort and reporting, this *FY 2014 Annual Report on Sexual Assault in the Military* provides an update on some information first disclosed in the *Report to the President.* In addition, this report includes an overview of the Department's FY 2014 SAPR programmatic and policy enhancements, a summary of completed Secretary of Defense-directed initiatives, and an update on the Department's efforts to comply with National Defense Authorization Act (NDAA) requirements, and final statistical data and analyses of reports of sexual assault involving Service members and case dispositions from FY 2014.

Oversight Actions

Eliminating sexual assault in the military is one of DoD's highest priorities. The Secretary of Defense and the Department leadership are committed to continually assessing and improving the Department's SAPR efforts. The DoD SAPR Office (SAPRO) is the single oversight body responsible for continuous assessment of the Department's SAPR strategy. SAPRO utilizes both qualitative and quantitative data collection and analysis methods, including surveys, focus groups, and sexual assault reporting data to evaluate the effectiveness of the Department's overall SAPR programs. The Secretaries of the Military Departments and the NGB also perform Service-specific internal assessments.

To foster program consistency and unity of effort across the Military Services and the NGB, the Director of DoD SAPRO continued to host regular SAPR Integrated Product Team (IPT) meetings with DoD and Military Service SAPR leadership.[27] The SAPR IPT provides a forum for the oversight of program execution, policy matters, and sharing of important research and best practices. In FY 2014, the SAPR IPT guided the development of policies and programs to comply with new legislation and initiatives from the Secretary of Defense.

DoD Sapr Strategic Plan

The *DoD SAPR Strategic Plan* defines the Department's SAPR priorities, objectives, and initiatives. In FY 2013, DoD SAPRO revised the *DoD SAPR Strategic Plan* to align with and operationalize the key tasks defined in the Joint Chiefs of Staff's (JCS) Strategic Direction to the Joint Force.[28] The *DoD SAPR Strategic Plan* presents a proactive and multidisciplinary approach with initiatives and objectives in five LOEs to achieve unity of effort and purpose across the Department in reducing, with a goal of eliminating, sexual assault. The LOEs outlined in Figure 3, are:

- Prevention;
- Investigation;
- Accountability;
- Advocacy/Victim Assistance; and
- Assessment.

The *DoD SAPR Strategic Plan* also contains 89 tasks, organized by LOEs, to be completed within four different timelines: Short (0-1 Year), Medium (1-2 Years), Long (2-3 Years), and Continual (Ongoing/Cyclical). Of the 89 original tasks, the Department completed 24 of 25 short-term tasks, as well as 4 medium-term tasks by the end of FY 2014. The tasks completed in FY 2014 are presented in this report, and the Department continues to work on the completing the in progress tasks. The *DoD SAPR Strategic Plan* was reviewed and updated during the beginning of January 2015.

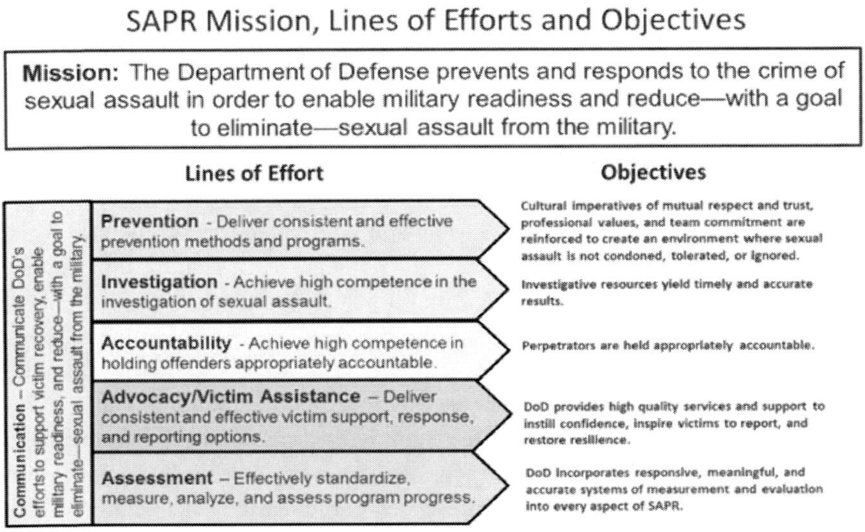

Figure 3. The Lines of Effort and Objectives of the *2013 DoD SAPR Strategic Plan.*

Secretary of Defense Initiatives

From FY 2012 to FY 2014, the Secretary of Defense directed 41 initiatives that fundamentally reformed how the military prevents, responds to, and adjudicates sexual assault. In FY 2014 alone, the Secretary of Defense directed 12 of the 41 initiatives. The initiatives have rapidly advanced substantial changes to the Department's approach to prevention and response. The efforts have included promoting a healthy command climate, enhancing training across all LOEs, revising SAPR policies and strategy regarding victim rights and care, and improving accountability measures for investigations and the military justice process. The Department works diligently to comply with the directives issued by the Secretary of Defense. By the end of the FY 2014, 6 initiatives were in progress. Many of the Secretary of Defense initiatives have been codified in NDAAs.

Outside Evaluations

To further improve the SAPR program, the Department supported the following outside evaluations during FY 2014.

The Response Systems to Adult Sexual Assault Crimes Panel

Section 576 of the NDAA for FY 2013[29] directed Secretary of Defense to establish the Response Systems to Adult Sexual Assault Crimes Panel (RSP) "to conduct an independent review and assessment of the systems used to investigate, prosecute, and adjudicate crimes involving adult sexual assault and related offenses under section 920 of title 10, United States Code (U.S.C.) (Article 120 of the Uniform Code of Military Justice (UCMJ)), for the purpose of developing recommendations regarding how to improve the effectiveness of such systems." The RSP released its report, including 132 recommendations for DoD, on June 27, 2014. During the latter half of FY 2014 and the beginning of FY 2015, the Department evaluated and approved the majority of RSP recommendations. In FY 2015, the Department will implement the approved recommendations and recommendations approved in part, and continue its assessment of the remaining recommendations. The status of the RSP recommendations will be reported in the FY 2015 Annual Report.

Government Accountability Office

Since 2008, the Government Accountability Office (GAO) has published the findings and recommendations from engagements evaluating DoD SAPR policies, programs, and functions. In September 2014, GAO published its report on actions taken to prevent sexual assault during initial military training and made five recommendations to the Department.[30] To date, DoD has implemented 26 of 32 recommendations from the engagements and is working to implement the remaining 6. Five of the six come from the report on preventing sexual assault during initial military training, and an update on meeting two of the five are provided in the Department of the Air Force (AF) Report at Enclosure 3. Additionally, at the end of FY 2014, there were two ongoing GAO assessments: an assessment of policies and programs pertaining to male victims of sexual assault and a review of DoD's efforts to prevent sexual assault. The GAO provided its report on policies and programs pertaining to male victims in March 2015 and its report on DoD's prevention efforts are due later in FY 2015.

PROGRAM AND POLICY ENHANCEMENTS

In FY 2014, the Department implemented numerous SAPR policy and program enhancements to its multi-disciplinary approach to combatting sexual assault. Many of these initiatives, program improvements, and policy enhancements were also presented in the *Report to the President*, which provided a detailed 3-year overview of the Department's SAPR efforts. This report highlights the progress made on these initiatives during FY 2014 and provides page references to the *Report to the President,* where applicable, for more information.

Line of Effort 1: Prevention Programs and Initiatives

Sexual assault prevention efforts advance a culture of dignity and respect for all who serve. Service members are at the heart of the Department's efforts; they are empowered to safely act when they see inappropriate behaviors and situations at risk for sexual assault. The desired end state for the Prevention LOE is to reinforce the cultural imperatives of mutual respect and trust, professional values, and team commitment to create an environment where sexist behaviors, sexual harassment, and sexual assault are not condoned, tolerated, or ignored.

The primary outcome measure associated with prevention efforts is a change in the past-year prevalence of the crime. Given the wide variety of prevention initiatives underway across the Department, it is difficult to identify which are having an impact on the occurrence of the crime. In fact, no entity or institution has been able to identify or prescribe a scientifically supported course of action that prevents sexual assault. Nonetheless, past Department research suggests that sexual assault tends to occur less frequently in military units where sexual harassment and other disrespectful behaviors are less prevalent.[31] Consequently, Department efforts, such as the Advance and Sustain Appropriate Culture and Review of Alcohol Policies initiatives, focus on enhancing climates of dignity and respect, empowering military members to identify and intervene in situations at risk for sexual assault, giving leadership the tools to regularly assess unit climate, and holding leadership appropriately accountable for their unit climates.

According to the *2014 RMWS,* the estimated percentage of surveyed active duty women who experienced unwanted sexual contact (USC)[32] in the past year declined from 6.1% in 2012 to 4.3% in 2014, a statistically significant decrease. For active duty men, the prevalence rate of USC trended downwards from 1.2% in 2012 to 0.9% in 2014.[33] Based on these prevalence rates, it is estimated that 18,900 Service members experienced USC, down from the 26,000 estimated in 2012. Although USC rates in 2014 are down significantly from those observed in 2006, the rates observed this year are about what they were in 2010. To achieve further progress, the Department must sustain the downward trend in prevalence rates in subsequent years. As a result, continued focus on sexual assault prevention remains a priority.

According to the *2014 RMWS*, an experience of past year sexual assault is highly correlated with an experience of past year sexual harassment. Compared to those who did not experience sexual harassment, those who did experience such incidents were more likely (14 times more likely among female Service members and 49 times more likely among male Service members) to experience sexual assault in the past year. Furthermore, about a third of Service member victims indicated that the alleged perpetrator(s) sexually harassed them before the sexual assault and a third indicated that the alleged perpetrator(s) sexually harassed them after the assault. Correlations were also found between gender discrimination and sexual assault. Sexual assault and sexual harassment are co-occurring problems that require continued DoD attention. An overview of these and other *RMWS* findings can be found in Annex 1 of this report.

Completed Prevention Strategic Plan Tasks

In FY 2014, the Department completed the following prevention tasks presented in the *DoD SAPR Strategic Plan*:

- Updated and published the DoD Sexual Assault Prevention Strategy;[34] and
- Developed a military community of practice (CoP) focused on primary prevention of sexual assault.

Secretary of Defense Prevention Initiatives

Secretary of Defense Prevention Initiatives

Standardize Protections	In progress	
Advance and Sustain Appropriate Culture	In progress	
Review Alcohol Policies	In progress	
Develop Collaborative Forum for Sexual Assault Prevention	Complete	
Training	Complete	

Complete
In progress
No Progress

The enhancements made in FY 2014 to meet the requirements of the Secretary of Defense prevention initiatives aim to deliver consistent and effective prevention methods and programs that reduce, with a goal to eliminate, sexual assault.

Standardize Protections

In August 2013, the Secretary of Defense ordered a review to ensure current policies prohibiting inappropriate relations between recruiters and recruits and trainers and trainees were consistent across the Military Services. This initiative was codified into law in the NDAA for FY 2014.[35] The Office of the Under Secretary of Defense for Personnel and Readiness (USD(P&R)) reviewed the pertinent policies. The Office of the USD(P&R) is drafting policy to address the issues identified.

Advance and Sustain Appropriate Culture

On May 1, 2014, to further enhance prevention programs, the Secretary of Defense directed the Secretaries of the Military Departments, in conjunction with the Chiefs of the Military Services and NGB, to update and integrate gender-responsive and culturally competent programs for leaders and Service members to address healthy relationships, active bystander intervention, social courage, and core values that support the establishment of mutual respect. In addition, the Secretary of Defense directed the Chiefs of Military Services to review policies that influence culture and behavior on military installations and in units and adjust policy within their purview, as appropriate.

Throughout FY 2014, the Military Departments and NGB worked to expand and revise gender-responsive and culturally competent programs aimed to advance and sustain appropriate culture. The Military Departments and NGB will brief the Secretary of Defense on implementation plans, methods, and recommendations in FY 2015.

Review Alcohol Policies

In May 2014, the Secretary of Defense directed the Military Departments and NGB to review and revise, as necessary, alcohol policies to address risk factors beyond the individual use of alcohol. This effort is designed to shape the environment for making responsible choices, and includes engaging with local community leaders, collaborating with off-post businesses to modify alcohol sales practices, and enhancing cooperation between the installation and the local community. The Military Departments and NGB will brief the Secretary of Defense on implementation plans, methods, and recommendations in FY 2015.

Develop Collaborative Forum for Sexual Assault Prevention

On May 1, 2014, the Secretary of Defense directed USD(P&R) to establish an implementation plan for a CoP to share promising prevention practices and lessons learned. In FY 2014, the Department established *DoD SAPR Connect,* which is the Department's collaboration and information-sharing CoP. *DoD SAPR Connect* has membership from all four Services and the National Guard, including many personnel from overseas locations. Additional details on the *DoD SAPR Connect CoP* can be found on pages 45-46 in the *Report to the President* and in the "FY 2014 Prevention Programmatic Highlights" portion below.

Evaluate Commander SAPR Training

On May 1, 2014, the Secretary of Defense directed the USD(P&R) to assess the effectiveness of the 2013 core competencies and learning objectives in pre-command and senior enlisted leader SAPR training to ensure all leaders are educated on sexual assault policies and provided the appropriate prevention tools.

In FY 2014, DoD officials observed a sample of each Service's pre-command and senior enlisted leader SAPR training and found progress in both the quality and the quantity of training since 2012. More information on SAPR training enhancements is provided on pages 52-53 in the *Report to the President.*

FY 2014 Prevention Programmatic Highlights

In addition to the Secretary of Defense initiatives, the Department implemented several other efforts in support of the Prevention LOE in FY 2014. This section provides highlights of the significant accomplishments.

Released 2014-2016 DoD Sexual Assault Prevention Strategy

On May 1, 2014, Secretary Hagel announced the *2014-2016 DoD Sexual Assault Prevention Strategy*, which provides a wide range of integrated programs to enhance the military environment, influence behavior, and reduce the occurrence of the crime. The strategy was informed by the work of civilian experts and is focused on shaping the environment where Service members live and work. The *Prevention Strategy* expands on the initial strategy published in 2008 and provides authoritative guidance on delivering consistent and effective prevention methods and programs for the Services. More detail on the *Prevention Strategy* can be found on pages 41-44 of the *Report to the President.*

Began Developing Guides to Prevent Sexual Assault in the Military

Recognizing that commanders have the responsibility to execute important components of the *Prevention Strategy*, DoD began developing a series of prevention guides targeted at all levels of command. The guides will be released in FY 2015 and FY 2016.

Developed DoD SAPR Connect CoP

In FY 2014, DoD developed a CoP to allow the Department to leverage and advance research, as well as share promising practices and lessons learned with external experts, federal partners, Military Services, advocacy organizations, and educational institutions for the prevention of sexual assault. *DoD SAPR Connect* is the Department's collaboration and information-sharing CoP. Comprised of four pillars (see Figure 4), *DoD SAPR Connect* leverages face-to-face meetings, virtual resources, webinars, and a community toolkit. *DoD SAPR Connect* involved participation from all four Services and the National Guard, including many personnel from overseas locations. By the end of FY 2014, *DoD SAPR Connect* had 332 members on the virtual platform, held its first prevention roundtable[36], and had an average of 221 participants in four webinars covering topics such as peer-to-peer mentorship, new soldier sponsorship, characteristics of sexual assault offenders, and the *DoD Sexual Assault Prevention Strategy.*

Figure 4. The Four Pillars of the *SAPR Connect CoP.*

Announced Prevention Innovation Award

In FY 2014, the Department announced the launch of the Sexual Assault Prevention Innovation Award to annually recognize groups or individuals (military or civilian) from each military component who have contributed or developed an innovative concept, methodology, or approach to positively impact sexual assault prevention efforts either on an installation, or in a deployed environment. The first awardees will be announced in FY 2015. More information on the 2014 Prevention Innovation Award is located on pages 54-55 of the *Report to the President.*

Figure 5. The 2014 SAAM Poster.

Observed Sexual Assault Awareness Month

In April 2014, the Department observed Sexual Assault Awareness Month (SAAM) with the theme "Live Our Values: Step Up to Stop Sexual Assault." The month offers an opportunity to build on existing momentum to fight the crime of sexual assault and to promote a culture of dignity and respect within the military community.

USD(P&R) encouraged the entire DoD community to raise awareness about the problem of sexual assault and its impact on mission readiness. Major General Jeffrey J. Snow, Director, SAPRO, visited troops at Fort Belvoir, Virginia, to kick off SAAM and described how important social courage and bystander intervention are in the Department's efforts to eliminate sexual assault.

SAAM also served as an opportunity to advertise the multi-disciplinary approach to prevention and victim advocacy, specifically the initiatives implemented by DoD in recent years to assist victims, including the DoD Safe Helpline, the Special Victims' Counsel (SVC)/Victims' Legal Counsel (VLC)[37] program, and the support offered by the Department's credentialed Sexual Assault Response Coordinators (SARC) and SAPR Victim Advocates (VA), among others. Major General Snow and Secretary of Defense Hagel also visited the DoD Safe Helpline office to commemorate SAAM and the anonymous hotline's 3rd Anniversary.

The 2014 Exceptional SARCs were recognized during SAAM for their outstanding efforts in assisting victims of sexual assault and for their commitment to preventing this crime. The 2014 awardees are:

- Army Master Sergeant Richard V. Fry, 21st Theater Sustainment Command, Germany;
- Ms. Shannon M. Moyer, Naval Air Station Lemoore, California;
- Ms. Midge M. Scott, Marine Corps Recruit Depot, Parris Island, South Carolina;
- Ms. Cindy W. Graver, Robins Air Force Base, Georgia;
- AF Major Katherine Maines, Joint Force Headquarters, Connecticut; and
- Mr. Christopher Hooper, 8th Coast Guard District, Missouri.

Further details on DoD's SAAM activities are on pages 53-54 of the *Report to the President.*

Line of Effort 2: Investigation Programs and Initiatives

Victim confidence and participation are integral to a thorough investigation. Investigative techniques that maximize the recovery of physical and testimonial evidence while minimizing the potential for victim re-traumatization benefit the military justice process. The purpose of the Investigation LOE is to ensure timely and accurate results.

Completed Investigation Strategic Plan Tasks

In FY 2014, the Department completed the following Investigation LOE tasks presented in the *DoD SAPR Strategic Plan*:

- Established the Special Victim Investigation and Prosecution (SVIP) capability;[38]
- Developed procedures to ensure early coordination between Military Criminal Investigative Organizations (MCIO) and Judge Advocates (JAs) when initiating sexual assault investigations;
- Established a Working Group to review initial baseline, periodic refresher, and advanced sexual assault investigation training in order

to establish common criteria, measures of effectiveness, and leverage training resources and expertise;

- Established SVIP case assessment protocol for open and closed sexual assault, child abuse, and domestic violence cases;
- Developed policy to ensure sexual assault documentation (DD Form 2911) is retained in accordance with NDAA for FY 2013; and
- Reviewed existing procedures to ensure all sexual assault allegations are referred to an MCIO.

Secretary of Defense Investigation Initiatives

Secretary of Defense Investigation Initiatives

	Action	Status
Ensure Investigative Quality	In progress (reoccurring)	░

● Complete

░ In progress

✖ No Progress

The objective of the Investigation LOE is achieving high competence in the investigation of sexual assault, and the Secretary of Defense initiative help to meet this objective.

Ensure Investigative Quality

In FY 2013, the DoD Inspector General (IG) completed its first evaluation of MCIO sexual assault investigations with adult victims to determine whether the MCIOs completed investigations as required by DoD, Military Service, and MCIO guidance. DoD IG found 89% of MCIO investigations closed (completed and adjudicated) in 2010 met investigative standards or had only minor deficiencies. DoD IG returned cases with significant deficiencies (11%) to the MCIOs for corrective action.

In August 2013, the Secretary of Defense requested DoD IG to evaluate the adequacy of closed sexual assault investigations on a recurring basis to ensure investigative quality.

In FY 2014, DoD IG evaluated MCIO adult sexual assault investigations that were initiated on or after January 1, 2012 and closed in FY 2013 to determine whether they were completed as required by DoD, Military Service, and MCIO guidance; the results of this evaluation were published in March 2015.[39]

In FY 2016, DoD IG plans to evaluate MCIO adult sexual assault investigations closed in 2015. Additionally, in FY 2016, DoD IG will gather data associated with any potential impact the SVC[40] program has had on investigations.

Figure 6. The DoD IG Seal.

FY 2014 Investigation Programmatic Highlights

In addition to the Secretary of Defense initiative, the Department implemented several other efforts in support of the Investigation LOE in FY 2014. This section provides highlights of the significant accomplishments.

Provided Report on SVIP Capability

On December 12, 2013, the Department provided a report to the Committees on Armed Services of the Senate and House of Representatives on the SVIP capability as required by section 573 of the NDAA for FY 2013.[41] The report described the Military Departments' plans and timelines for establishing SVIP capabilities, along with an assessment of those plans and timelines. The SVIP capability became fully operational in January 2014.

The report found that the Department's collective capability is organized differently in each Military Service:

- The Army assigned 23 Special Victim Prosecutors (SVP) dedicated to the handling of sexual assault and family violence cases. Army SVPs work with U.S. Army Criminal Investigation Command (CID) special agents and Special Victim Unit (SVU) investigative teams at over 65 installations worldwide to investigate and prosecute special victim offenses. The Army also retained several highly qualified experts (HQE) who have served as civilian criminal prosecutors to provide training, mentorship, and advice to JAs and CID special agents across the globe.

- The Navy has nine regional-based Senior Trial Counsel who collaborate with Naval Criminal Investigation Service (NCIS) special agents to investigate, review, and prosecute special victim cases. Those nine Senior Trial Counsels are all Military Justice Litigation Career Track qualified litigation specialists, and they supervise approximately 35 prosecutors worldwide. All nine regional prosecution departments have been specially trained and certified to prosecute adult sexual assault cases under the Navy's SVIP capability. The Navy also created a Trial Counsel Assistance Program (TCAP) with case review and prosecution reach-back and support capabilities. TCAP attorneys can also be detailed to prosecute complex cases. The Navy also has several civilian and HQE positions, through which civilian attorneys with extensive prosecution experience provide assistance to trial counsel in complex and sexual assault cases and specialized training.
- The Marine Corps established specially qualified, geographically assigned Complex Trial Teams comprised of 48 special qualified victim Trial Counsels and each led by a seasoned Regional Trial Counsel providing special victim prosecutorial expertise and support. The Marine Corps also established HQE positions, through which civilian attorneys with extensive litigation and court-martial experience provide assistance to trial counsel in complex and sexual assault litigation. Marine Corps JAs also team with NCIS special agents in special victim cases. Furthermore, the Marine Corps recently increased the opportunity for its JAs to receive graduate-level education in criminal law.
- The AF maintains a team of 16 Senior Trial Counsels (STC), including 10 who are members of the AF SVU-STC, working alongside 24 Air Force Office of Special Investigations (AFOSI) special agents located at 16 AF installations with a high number of reported sexual offenses. The AF has also established a reach-back capability situated at Joint Base Andrews, Maryland, which is comprised of the AFOSI Sexual Assault Investigation and Operations

Consultant and the Judge Advocate General Corps SVU Chief of Policy and Coordination, who provide expert assistance for investigators and JAs in the field.

- Additionally, the Department established criteria for measuring the effectiveness and impact of the SVIP capability from investigative, prosecutorial, and victim perspectives. The criteria are:
    - Percentage of SVIP cases preferred, compared to overall number of courts-martial preferred in each FY;
    - Percentage of special victim offense courts-martial tried by, or with the direct advice and assistance of, a specially trained prosecutor;
    - Compliance with DoD Victim Witness Assistance Program (VWAP) reporting requirements to ensure victims are consulted with and regularly updated by SVIP legal personnel;
    - Percentage of specially trained prosecutors and other legal support personnel having received additional and advanced training in SVIP topical areas; and
    - Victim feedback on the effectiveness of SVIP prosecution and legal support services and recommendations for possible improvements; participation by victims will be voluntary and provide for confidentiality to the extent allowed by law, feedback mechanisms will be coordinated and standardized within each Military Service so that victims do not have to unnecessarily complete multiple questionnaires, and these mechanisms will be used to gain a greater understanding of the reasons why a victim who filed an Unrestricted Report elected or declined to participate at trial and whether SVIP prosecution and legal support services had any positive impact on this decision.[42]
- Each Service provided FY 2014 data for these measures of effectiveness and can be found in their annual reports, which are enclosures to this report.

To foster growth in the SVIP Capability and SVC programs, Congress appropriated $25M in FY 2014 for expanding the Department's competencies in investigation and prosecution of allegations of sexual offenses.[43] Funding was distributed to the Military Services to improve training and resourcing of attorneys serving as SVCs, help increase reporting, improve victim assistance, enhance investigative capability, and ultimately improve victim confidence in the Department's comprehensive response system.

> Who are the SVIP capability team members?
>
> *MCIO Investigators*
> *VWAP Personnel*
> *Paralegal Support Personnel*
> *Trial Counsels*

Improved Training in Support of SVIP Capability Implementation

Also in FY 2014, the Department developed and issued investigative and legal policies to implement the SVIP capability. DoD IG developed policy and procedures for the MCIOs for the implementation of SVIP capability in the Directive-type Memorandum (DTM) 14-002 – "The Establishment of Special Victim Capability within the Military Criminal Investigative Organizations."[44] According to DTM 14-002, the selection of MCIO investigators for the SVIP capability is contingent on their completion of specialized training. At a minimum, DTM 14-002 requires this training to cover the following competencies:

- Legal jurisdiction for conducting criminal investigations;
- Elements of proof for SVIP covered offenses;
- Crime scene management;
- Deoxyribonucleic Acid (DNA) collection requirements;
- Identifying, obtaining, preserving, and transporting forensic evidence;
- Rights of crime victims and available victim and witness assistance, support, and counseling services available;
- Sensitivities associated with child abuse victims, including but not limited to interviewing techniques, Sexual Assault Forensic Examination (SAFE) kits, risk factors, and protective orders; and
- Sensitivities associated with victims of sexual assault, including but not limited to interviewing techniques, impact of trauma, SAFE kits and medical treatment, counseling, victim support, establishing victim trust and transparency, impact of alcohol and drugs, and protective orders.

The Office of Legal Policy developed policy and procedures for SVIP legal personnel in DTM 14-003, "DoD Implementation of Special Victim Capability Prosecution and Legal Support."[45] DTM 14-003 establishes the standards for the selection, certification, and training of SVIP prosecutors and legal support personnel and outlines the training program for SVIP prosecutors, which must include:

- The elements of proof for SVIP offenses;
- Effective interviewing techniques and the impact of trauma on memory;
- Legal issues and sensitivities associated with sexual assault victims;
- Legal issues and sensitivities associated with child abuse victims; and
- Legal issues and sensitivities associated with victims of domestic violence;

The Department's SVIP capability program is also discussed on pages 66-68 and pages 81-82 of the *Report to the President.*

DoD IG Evaluated MCIOs' Sexual Assault Investigation Policies

In September 2014, DoD IG published findings and recommendations for the MCIOs in its report, *Evaluation of the Military Criminal Investigative Organizations' Adult Sexual Assault Investigation Policies.*[46] DoD IG evaluated the MCIOs' policies and procedures to determine whether they aligned with DoD and Military Service mandates, as well as Council for Inspectors General on Integrity and Efficiency (CIGIE) Quality Standards for Investigations (QSI) and generally accepted law enforcement adult sexual assault investigative techniques.

DoD IG found that the MCIOs' adult sexual assault investigation policies and procedures support each agency's need for a thorough sexual assault investigation. The MCIOs have incorporated nearly all DoD and Service adult sexual assault investigative requirements into their policies. Although not mandated by DoD, the MCIOs have also incorporated, directly or indirectly, the pertinent CIGIE QSIs relating to conducting criminal investigations, including sexual assault, and those that facilitate a thorough and well-written report of investigation. The MCIOs address almost all of the pertinent International Association of Chiefs of Police (IACP) investigative actions in their policies.

DoD IG issued four recommendations in its report. It recommended that the MCIOs evaluate IACP adult sexual assault investigative techniques identified as not currently aligned within MCIO policy for their relevance and applicability and consider incorporating them into their adult sexual assault investigation policy guidance. Secondly, the report recommended that the Director, NCIS and the Commander, AFOSI evaluate their procedures addressing actions to be taken relating to victim collateral misconduct in a sexual assault investigation. Furthermore, it recommended that the Director, NCIS and the Commander, AFOSI evaluate the benefits and efficiencies of including DoD and Service sexual assault investigative policy in MCIO policies. Finally, DoD IG recommended that the Director, NCIS evaluate the policy verbiage related to the discussion of the victim preference statement with the victim, specifically, the language used to demonstrate a possible consequence of a victim's decision not to cooperate, to eliminate implied victim blaming.

Line of Effort 3: Accountability Programs and Initiatives

Achieving high competence in holding alleged offenders appropriately accountable is the objective of the Accountability LOE. The program enhancements implemented in FY 2014 under the Accountability LOE aim to achieve this objective.

Completed Accountability Strategic Plan Tasks

In FY 2014, the Department completed the following tasks presented in the *DoD SAPR Strategic Plan*:

- Enhanced sexual assault training for attorneys and military judges;
- Conducted assessment of DoD Pilot Program for SVC;
- Established and supported independent review and assessment panels required under the section 576 of the NDAA for FY 2013;
- Expanded the availability, sequencing, and scope of commanders' legal courses across the Services;
- Assessed effectiveness of the policy to elevate initial disposition authority in certain sexual assault cases to commanders, in the grade of O-6 or higher, who possess Special Court-Martial Convening Authority;
- Updated policies on separation of sexual offenders; and

- Increased SAPR first responder knowledge of Military Rule of Evidence (MRE) 514 (Victim Advocate-Victim Privilege).

Secretary of Defense Accountability Initiatives

Secretary of Defense Accountability Initiatives

	Action	Status
Assess Military Justice Systems	Complete	●
Improve Victims' Counsel	Complete	●
Improve Victim Legal Support	Complete	●
Enhance Pretrial Investigation	Complete	●

● Complete

In progress

✖ No Progress

The Department strives for a fair and equitable system of accountability that promotes justice and assists in maintaining good order and discipline. The Secretary of Defense Accountability Initiatives uphold and enhance the ways in which the military justice system encourages victim participation, while maintaining the rights of the accused.

Assess Military Justice Systems

In May 2013, the Secretary of Defense called upon the RSP[47] to accelerate its review and provide final recommendations within 12 months of the panel's first meeting. This initiative[48] was codified into law with the NDAA for FY 2014.[49]

In June 2014, RSP delivered its final report to the Secretary and Committees on Armed Services of the Senate and House of Representatives, which included 132 recommendations. After careful consideration, Secretary Hagel approved the majority of the recommendations, 88 full recommendations and 10 in part, and disapproved 1 recommendation.[50] Of the remaining, 6 were referred to working groups for further study, 11 are under review by the Joint Services Committee on Military Justice, and 16 are under consideration by the Military Justice Review group.[51]

The USD(P&R) is responsible for overseeing the RSP recommendation implementation and is the office of primary responsibility for 59 recommendations. In FY 2014, the Department reviewed all 132 recommendations and provided an office of primary responsibility and, if necessary, an office of coordinating responsibility for all approved recommendations. After an initial review of the recommendations, DoD determined that the following 10 recommendations were already implemented:

- Develop/implement military crime victimization survey;
- Utilize the results from the *Workplace and Gender Relations Survey of Active Duty Members (WGRA)* to assess attitudes, identify areas for improvement, and revise workplace policies;
- Analyze raw data collected from surveys using independent research professionals to assess how DoD can improve responses to sexual assault;
- Use UCMJ definitions of sexual assault offenses in military crime victimization surveys;
- Refrain from additional formal statements of what accountability, rights, and responsibilities a member of the Armed Forces has with regard to matters of sexual assault prevention and response;
- Ensure sexual assault reporting options are clarified for all members of the military;
- Clarify that DoD Safe Helpline is the single military 24/7 sexual assault crisis hotline for Service members;
- Establish an easily remembered DoD Safe Helpline number similar to website name;
- Continue training all levels of law enforcement personnel on potential biases and inaccurate perceptions of victim behavior; and
- Maintain the requirement for an investigator to notify the prosecution section of the Staff Judge Advocate legal office of an Unrestricted Report as soon as practicable, but no later than 24 hours.

A major area of focus for the RSP was assessing the role of the commander in the military justice system. The RSP concluded that military justice system reforms should not include removing prosecutorial discretion from military commanders. As the RSP found: "The evidence does not support a conclusion that removing convening authority from senior commanders will reduce the incidence of sexual assault, increase reporting of sexual assaults, or improve the quality of investigations and prosecutions of sexual assault cases in the Armed Forces."[52] Additional DoD discussion of the RSP and its report can be found on pages 34-35 and pages 88-89 of the *Report to the President.*

Improve Victims' Counsel

In May 2013, the Secretary of Defense directed an evaluation of the AF SVC pilot program to ensure that victims are provided advice and assistance they need to understand their rights and to feel confident in the military justice system. The AF began its SVC pilot program in January 2013. SVCs are Active Duty JAs whose role is to represent victims in an attorney-client relationship in the investigation and court-martial process. Sexual assault victims are assigned an SVC within 48 hours (when practicable) of the SVC Program Office receiving a request.

Figure 7. U.S Air Force Special Victims' Counsel Program Received 2014 Federal Service Award.

The Department published its report in FY 2014 and found that the SVC pilot program was well received by victims who used its services. The report provided the results from a victim impact survey that was fielded by the Military Justice Division, AF Legal Operations Agency on March 20, 2013. The survey found:

- 90% were "extremely satisfied" with the advice and support the SVC provided during the Article 32 hearing and court-martial;
- 98% would recommend other victims request an SVC;

- 91% indicated their SVC advocated effectively on their behalf; and
- 94% indicated their SVC helped them understand the investigation and court-martial processes.

Improve Victim Legal Support

Due to the benefits observed in the AF SVC program, the Secretary of Defense directed the Secretaries of the Military Departments in August 2013 to establish a special victims' advocacy program to provide legal advice and representation to victims throughout the military justice process.

Each Service reached full operational capability in January 2014. This Secretary of Defense initiative[53] was codified in section 1716 of the NDAA for FY 2014. Additional details of the SVC program are found on pages 78-81 of the *Report to the President.*

Enhance Pretrial Investigations

In his August 2013 memorandum, the Secretary of Defense directed the Secretaries of the Military Services to implement policy, mandating JAs serve as investigating officers for all Article 32 hearings on sexual assault offense charges. Section 1702 of the NDAA for FY 2014 contained a provision generally requiring that, starting in late 2014, preliminary hearing officers presiding over Article 32 hearings are to be JAs. Unlike that provision, the Secretary of Defense's policy allows for no exceptions to the JA requirement in sexual assault offense cases. As of December 3, 2013, all the Military Departments complied with this requirement. This initiative is also discussed on page 84 of the *Report to the President.*

FY 2014 Accountability Programmatic Highlights

In addition to the Secretary of Defense initiatives, the Department implemented several other efforts in support of the Accountability LOE in FY 2014. This section provides highlights of the significant accomplishments.

DoD IG Evaluated DoD Compliance with the Sex Offender Registration and Notification Act

On August 29, 2014, DoD IG concluded an evaluation of the Department's compliance with the Sex Offender Registration and Notification Act (SORNA), established by Title I of the "Adam Walsh Child Protection and Safety Act of 2006" (P.L. 109-248).[54] It also evaluated whether the Department effectively accounted for registered sex offenders with access to

DoD facilities. DoD IG found the Department was compliant with SORNA registration requirements. However, DoD IG recommended a number of actions to improve reporting, accountability, and monitoring of registered sex offenders within the Department. Overall USD (P&R) and the Secretaries of the Military Departments management comments were responsive and agreed with our recommendations.

Updated Policies on Separation of Sexual Offenders

In FY 2014, the Services reviewed and updated their policies, as necessary, to ensure that Service members who have been convicted for a sexual assault, but not adjudged a punitive discharge, are entered into administrative discharge proceedings by the Military Services.

- In November 2013, the Secretary of the Army issued Army Directive 2013-21, "Initiating Separation Proceedings and Prohibiting Overseas Assignment for Soldiers Convicted of Sex Offenses," to require the initiation of separation proceedings for any Soldier convicted of a sex offense. Decisions to retain enlisted Soldiers convicted of a sex offense are referred for the exercise of Secretarial plenary authority under Army Regulation 635-200, "Active Duty Enlisted Administrative Separations."
- The Department of the Navy (DON) has official policies in the Navy and the Marine Corps to ensure that Service members who have been convicted for a sexual assault, but not adjudged a punitive discharge, are entered into administrative discharge proceedings.
    - The Navy was already compliant with this requirement. In May 2009, the Office of the Chief of Naval Operations (OPNAV) issued Instruction 1752.3, "Policy for Sex Offender Tracking, Assignment, and Access Restrictions within the Navy," which provides guidance on separation of sexual assault offenders. Additionally, Military Personnel Manual 1900-040, "Transfer to the Retired List, Retired Reserve, or the Fleet Reserve in a Restricted Status," issued in September 2008, prohibits a convicted sex offender from entering any installation, facility, or property under the cognizance of DON.
    - In November 2013, DON issued Marine Corps Order 1900.16, "Separation and Retirement Manual," requiring mandatory processing for separation following the first substantiated incident, or substantiated attempted incident, of sexual

misconduct. Also, in June 2014, DON issued All Navy 050/14, "Implementation of Section 1705 of the NDAA for FY 2014 Related to Court-Martial Jurisdictional Limits and Minimum Sentences for Certain Sex Offenses," which requires mandatory dismissal or dishonorable discharge for convictions for certain sex offenses.

- AF was also in compliance with this requirement. Change 7, issued in 2004, to AF Instructions 36-3206, "Administrative Discharge Procedures for Commissioned Officers," and 36-3208, "Administrative Discharge of Airmen," mandate initiation of discharge proceedings for any member who has committed sexual assault.

Increased SAPR First Responder Knowledge of MRE 514 (Victim Advocate-Victim Privilege)

In FY 2014, each of the Services worked to increase first responder knowledge of MRE 514, Victim-Victim Advocate privilege. Subject to certain exceptions, MRE 514 provides a victim with the privilege to refuse to disclose and to prevent any other person from disclosing a confidential communication made between the victim and a SARC and SAPR VA, in a case arising under the UCMJ, if the communication was made for the purpose of facilitating advice or supportive assistance to the victim.[55]

- The Army SARC and SAPR VA certification training includes significant blocks of instruction on MRE 514.
- MRE 514 awareness training is covered in the 40-hour training required for Navy SARCs and SAPR VAs to earn initial certification and re-certification.
- A separate MRE 514 brief is included in the mandatory 40-hour SAPR VA training for Marine Corps SAPR personnel and is taught by a judge advocate. Additional training is provided in all iterations of customized SARC training to facilitate practical application of MRE 514.
- All AF SARCs and SAPR VAs attend the SARC Course at Maxwell Air Force Base. The course includes a lesson on MRE 514, which encompasses a thorough explanation of the victim advocate-victim privilege by a JA.

Line of Effort 4: Advocacy/Victim Assistance Programs and Initiatives

In the Department, sexual assault victims are offered and provided advocacy services, medical care, counseling, legal assistance, victim witness assistance, and chaplain services. Critical to successful advocacy and victim assistance are trained and knowledgeable professionals who are known and available to Service members and whose services and programs facilitate victim reporting.

Completed Advocacy/Victim Assistance Strategic Plan Tasks

In FY 2014, the Department completed the following tasks presented in the *DoD SAPR Strategic Plan*:

- Assessed and improved portability of victim services in deployed environments;
- Developed policy to ensure victims are provided appropriate rights, protections, and services and extend crime victims' rights to victims of offenses under the UCMJ; and
- DoD IG Investigations of allegations of retaliatory personnel actions taken.

Secretary of Defense Advocacy/Victim Assistance Initiatives

Secretary of Defense Advocacy/Victim Assistance Initiatives

	Action	Status
Improve Response and Victim Treatment	Complete	●
Ensure Victim's Rights	In progress	■
Expand Victim Rights	Complete	●
Enhance Protections	Complete	●
Sensitive Position Screening	Complete	●
Improve Response for Male Victims	In progress	■

● Complete

■ In progress

✖ No Progress

The objective for the Advocacy/Victim Assistance LOE is to deliver consistent and effective victim support, response, and reporting options. The actions taken to meet the requirements of the Secretary of Defense Advocacy/Victim Assistance Initiatives enhance the Department's ability to provide effective victim support.

Improve Response and Victim Treatment

To improve victim care and trust in the chain of command, increase reporting, and reduce the possibility of ostracizing victims, Secretary of Defense directed the Secretaries of the Military Departments to implement and monitor methods to improve victim treatment by peers, co-workers, and chains of command.

Secretary of Defense instructed Military Departments to solicit victim input for the development of these methods. The Army utilized discussion groups led by the Vice Chief of Staff and gave victims the opportunity to speak at its semi-annual SHARP Command Summit. The DON used surveys and in-person meetings with victims to solicit input. The AF provided survivors with the opportunity to assist with developing training curriculum.

Ensure Victim's Rights

In May 2013, the Secretary of Defense directed OGC to develop a method to incorporate the rights afforded to victims through the Crime Victims' Rights Act (18 U.S.C.) 3771) (CVRA) into military justice practice, to the extent appropriate. Section 1701 of the NDAA for FY 2014 extended similar rights to those presented in CVRA, aligning military justice practice with federal civilian CVRA. In FY 2015, the Department is slated to forward a recommendation to the President on relevant changes for the Manual for Courts-Martial (MCM).[56] Ensuring victim rights is also discussed in the *Report to the President* on page 84.

Expand Victim Rights

In his August 2013 memorandum, the Secretary of Defense directed DoD General Counsel to develop a recommendation for an Executive Order to amend the MCM to provide victims the opportunity to have input to the post-trial action phase of courts-martial, in order to ensure that victims have a voice throughout the entire justice process. The DoD General Counsel's recommendation was incorporated into an Executive Order published on June 13, 2014.[57]

Enhance Protections

The Secretary of Defense ordered the Secretaries of the Military Departments in FY 2013 to develop and implement policy allowing the administrative reassignment or transfer of a Service member who is accused of committing a sexual offense, providing enhanced victim protection and balancing the interests of the victim and the alleged offender. In FY 2014, the Military Services reviewed, updated as necessary, and briefed their respective policies to conform to the Secretary of Defense's initiative.

- The Army was already compliant with this requirement. The Department of the Army issued the "Expedited Transfer or Reassignment Procedures for Victims of Sexual Assault" directive on October 3, 2011.
  - This directive allows Army commanders to conduct expedited transfer for members who are either the victim of a sexual assault or accused of committing a sexual assault or related offense, if they deem such action is in the best interests of both the victim and the accused.
- The DON has official policies in the Navy and the Marine Corps regarding the administrative reassignment or transfer of both victims of sexual assault and those accused of committing sexual assault.
  - The Navy was also in compliance with this requirement. The OPNAV Instruction 1752.1B, "Navy Sexual Assault Victim Intervention Program," issued in 2006, includes guidance in sexual assault cases to relocate the victim or alleged offender until the case is legally settled and/or the victim is considered out of danger when the victim and alleged offender are assigned to the same command.
  - The Marine Admin Message 031/14 "Administrative Reassignment or Transfer of Marines Accused of Sexual Assault or Related Offense," signed in January 2014, provided implementing guidance to commanders on the consideration of, and processes for, transfer of members accused of sexual assault or a related offense.
- The Department of the AF issued the AF Guidance Memorandum (AFGM) to AF Instruction (AFI) 36-2110 "Assignments" on January 1, 2014. This AFGM to AFI 36-2110 incorporates new guidelines for the reassignment of AF members who were sexually assaulted and

approved for expedited transfer, as well as for the reassignment of AF alleged offenders accused of sexual assault or related offense.

These policies also fulfill the requirements outlined in the NDAA for FY 2014.[58]

Sensitive Position Screening

On 23 June 2014, the Secretary of Defense approved four recommendations to enhance screening, selection, training, and/or certification/licensure for personnel assigned to those sensitive positions in which they directly engage, support, or instruct the newest and most vulnerable Service members:

- SARC and SAPR VAs;
- Recruiters;
- Healthcare providers performing SAFE;
- Initial entry/basic training instructors for officers and enlisted Service members;
- MCIO investigators who conduct criminal investigations and support the DoD SVIP capability;
- SVIP capability legal team: prosecutors, paralegals, and VWAP personnel selected to support the SVIP capability; and
- SVC.

Background information regarding this initiative is discussed on page 120 of the *Report to the President.*

Improve Response for Male Victims

In May 2014, the Secretary of Defense directed the Secretaries of the Military Departments, in conjunction with the Chiefs of the Military Services and NGB, to implement and monitor methods to improve reporting and enhance efforts to encourage male victims to seek assistance. The Military Departments are to solicit male victim input in the development of these methods. The Military Departments were directed to provide implementation plans and methods in FY 2015. Additional information about male victims is provided in Appendix C of this report.

FY 2014 Advocacy/Victim Assistance Programmatic Highlights

In addition to the Secretary of Defense initiatives, the Department implemented several other efforts in support of the Advocacy/Victim Assistance LOE in FY 2014. This section provides highlights of significant accomplishments.

Issued Guidance on Retention of DD Form 2910 and DD 2911

Section 1723 of the NDAA for FY 2014 mandated the retention of Department of Defense (DD) Form 2910, *Victim Reporting Preference Statement*, and DD Form 2911, *DoD Sexual Assault Forensic Examination Report* for 50 years, in order to maintain an additional record of the sexual assault report, regardless of the type of report or whether such retention was requested by the victim.[59] In July 2014, the USD(P&R) issued a memorandum to the Services and NGB directing they implement interim policy to immediately meet the NDAA requirement as DoD develops a long-term solution. The Department will issue a change to DoD Instruction (DoDI) 6495.02, "SAPR Program Procedures" to capture this retention requirement.

Figure 8. RAINN Director Scott Berkowitz gives Secretary of Defense Hagel a tour of the Safe Helpline facility in April 2014.

Sustained the DoD Safe Helpline

The DoD Safe Helpline is a confidential, anonymous crisis support service for the DoD community affected by sexual assault. Safe Helpline provides live, one-on-one expert advice, information, and resources for survivors of sexual assault. Available 24/7 globally, users can "click, call or text" for anonymous and confidential support.[60]

The number of new visitors to the Safe Helpline website in FY 2014 was a 47% increase from the number of new visitors in FY 2013, and a 330% increase from the number of new visitors in FY 2012. This increase in visits largely reflects Department efforts to publicize the service. This increased visibility is essential so that survivors and others in the DoD community can access help and get information when and where they need it. Website visitors may directly search the Safe Helpline database of SARCs and other first responders in order to find referral and contact information. From FY 2013 to FY 2014 the number of searches increased by 214%.

From FY 2013 to FY 2014, the total number of Safe Helpline phone user contacts increased by 70%, and the total number of online user contacts increased by 25%. In FY 2014, 5,984 phone users and 2,513 online users contacted the Safe Helpline. The most frequently discussed topics for both male and female users were reporting options, emotional and social consequences of the assault, and mental health services. In FY 2014, nearly half of users who discussed a sexual assault event also discussed barriers to reporting.[61] User satisfaction with the Safe Helpline continues to remain high. Average feedback ratings are consistently over 4.0 on scale from 1 (strongly disagree) to 5 (strongly agree).Additional information illustrating the variety of referrals and the importance that SARCs and other military support staff play in providing services to Safe Helpline users can be found in Appendix F.

Certified Additional SARCs and SAPR VAs

The Department fully implemented the DoD Sexual Assault Advocate Certificate Program (D-SAACP) in FY 2013. In FY 2014, the program played an important role in ensuring DoD victim assistance and advocacy professionals provide a consistent, high standard of quality care to survivors of sexual assault. D-SAACP provides survivors with the assurance that their SARC and SAPR VA have undergone a rigorous review, are knowledgeable about resources and services, and are equipped to provide victim advocacy within the military structure. Since the program was launched in FY 2012, over 35,000 SARCs and SAPR VAs have been certified through the D-SAACP process. In FY 2014 alone, over 13,000 SARCs and SAPR VAs were certified. Additional information on the D-SAACP program can be found on pages 106-109 of the *Report to the President.*

Sustained Survivor Meeting

In place since 2010, the biannual Survivor Meetings provide the SAPRO Director with the opportunity to speak directly with victims of sexual assault who have reported the incident within the previous three years. Direct victim feedback in this venue provides insights into the toll this crime takes on its victims and the DoD community. This feedback enables SAPRO to see how SAPR policy and Service program execution affect the individual. In FY 2014, the Survivor Meetings took place in March and September and were attended by a total of 12 survivors (male and female), from each Service and NGB.

Increased Reporting

It is the Department's goal to not only prevent sexual assault, but also to increase the proportion of victims who choose to report. Reporting allows victims to engage restorative care and services. In addition, it allows the Department to hold offenders appropriately accountable. While the estimated prevalence of the crime is down from FY 2012 to FY 2014, the overall reporting of sexual assault in the same period increased substantially. Reporting increased by 53% from FY 2012 to FY 2013, and increased by another 11% from FY 2013 to FY 2014.

In FY 2014, 5,284 Service member victims made an Unrestricted or Restricted Report. Of the 5,284 Service member victims, there were 516 who made a report of sexual assault for an incident occurring prior to military service and 4,768 who made a report for an incident that occurred during military service.

The 4,768 Service members who made a sexual assault report in FY 2014 for an incident that occurred during military service accounted for approximately 25% of the estimated number of Service members who may have experienced unwanted sexual contact. Thus, DoD estimates that it received a report from 1 in 4 military victims of sexual assault in 2014, up from just 1 in 10 in 2012.

While DoD would like all victims to consider reporting the crime, the Department respects a victim's right not to choose to report. Consequently, victims may access the DoD Safe Helpline to speak anonymously with specially trained personnel who can provide them with crisis intervention, information, and resources 24 hours a day, 365 days a year. In addition, Restricted Reporting continues as a trusted option for confidentially accessing support and services, without having to participate in a criminal investigation or the military justice process. Victims who file a Restricted Report also have the option to convert to an Unrestricted Report. Over time, the percentage of victims who convert their Restricted Reports to Unrestricted Reports has remained relatively stable with an average of 15%. However, in FY 2014, the conversion rate increased to 20%. Additional information about the reports received this year and historical trends are described in the *Statistical Data on Sexual Assault* (Appendix A) portion of this report.

Combatting Retaliation

One of the main goals of the Advocacy/Victim Assistance LOE is to instill confidence in victims to know that when they report a sexual assault, there is no reason to fear retaliation. While retaliation of any kind is prohibited within DoD, an appreciable portion of Service members in the *2014 RMWS* indicated experiencing social or professional retaliation associated with their sexual assault report. The Department asks about retaliation on surveys to better assess victims' wellbeing and to understand the stressors victims experience following a report of sexual assault. DoD collects this information in order to provide input to leadership to help them understand the destructive nature of retaliation. This information also helps the Department to adjust support programs and tailor services and training to match victims' needs, as well as to raise awareness about this issue with commanders. However, recent victims' survey responses indicate broad perceptions of alleged retaliation that may not necessarily align with actionable offenses that meet the elements of proof required for a charge of retaliation under military law. DoD fully recognizes that sexual assault is a highly underreported crime in the military (and society at large) and that the fear of retaliation is a barrier to reporting. While DoD seeks to remedy victims' perceptions of alienation by peers and reprisal by other parties, these perceptions are only one piece of a retaliation charge. Other factors, such as the intent of the individual suspected of reprisal and the behavior experienced by the victim, must be investigated before criminal offenses can be charged. Therefore, the Department employs a system that not only allows for handling retaliation allegations in the military justice system, but also with administrative actions that can address inappropriate behavior that falls short of the criminal elements of proof.

Figure 9. Sailors and Marines participate in a 5K run in support of Sexual Assault Awareness Month 2014 on the flight deck of the aircraft carrier USS Harry S. Truman.

In FY 2014, each Service implemented new regulations against retaliation and ostracism. Retaliation includes taking or threatening to take an adverse personnel action or withholding or threatening to withhold a favorable personnel action, with respect to a member of the Armed Forces because the member reported a criminal offense. Additionally, retaliation may include social ostracism and such acts of maltreatment, as designated by the Secretaries of the Military Departments, committed by peers of the victim or by other Service members because the member reported a criminal offense, made with the intent to deter reporting or otherwise impede the administration of justice.[62] Violation of Service regulations could result in criminal prosecution under Article 92 of the UCMJ – "Failure to Obey Orders or Regulation" and/or Article 93 – "Cruelty and Maltreatment." In addition, Service member victims can avail themselves of the following resources to report retaliation or ostracism:

- Report to their commander;
- Request an Expedited Transfer;
- Request a Safety Transfer, if they fear violence;
- Request a Military Protective Order and/or Civilian Protective Order;
- File a Military Equal Opportunity Complaint;
- Report to a SARC at a different installation;
- Report to a commander outside their Chain of Command; and
- Report to the DoD IG Defense Hotline.

Third parties can also file a DoD IG Defense Hotline complaint when they witness retaliation.

The Department identified retaliation associated with sexual assault reporting as one of its metrics for the *Report to the President*. This was based on the results from the *2012 WGRA* that indicated victims who reported the crime perceived social and professional retaliation associated with their report. In order to gain a better understanding of the scope of the problem, the Department assessed retaliation through multiple data sources, including:

- Defense Equal Opportunity Management Institute Organizational Climate Survey (DEOCS)
- The 2014 RMWS
- The 2014 SES

Command Climate Perspective

The *DEOCS* included six items to assess command climate perceptions associated with reporting of sexual assault and how those who make a report are viewed.[63] The items used a four-point scale ranging from "Not at all likely" to "Very likely." Overall, Service members who completed the *DEOCS* in 2014 perceived the potential for retaliation from their command and unit members to be unlikely (i.e. they perceived a favorable climate associated with reporting sexual assault). However, on average men (3.5 on a 4.0 scale) perceived a slightly more favorable reporting climate, with a lower likelihood of retaliation, compared to women (3.4 on a 4.0 scale). Moreover, senior enlisted Service members and officers (E7-E9, W1-W5, and O1 and above, respectively; 3.7 on a 4.0 scale) perceived that retaliation was less likely to occur compared to junior enlisted Service members and non-commissioned officers (E1-E3 and E4-E6, respectively; 3.4 on a 4.0 scale).

The 2014 RMWS

Of the 4.3% of women who indicated experiencing USC in the past year and who reported the matter to a military authority or organization, 62% perceived some form of professional or social retaliation, administrative action, and/or punishment associated with their report (53% social retaliation, 35% adverse administrative action, 32% professional retaliation, and 11% punishment for infraction). [64] However, because the data do not provide for the circumstances regarding administrative action or actions, which victims perceive as professional retaliation, we are unable to draw any conclusions regarding these numbers. Data for men were not reportable due to the small number of male respondents in this category.

The 2014 SES

In the *SES*, a similar pattern was observed, with 59% of respondents perceiving social retaliation and 40% of respondents perceiving professional retaliation. [65] The *SES* involves survivors who responded to an invitation to take the survey (a convenience sample). Nonetheless, the results on this item were comparable with results obtained through the *2014 RMWS*, giving a good indication that the respondents to the *SES* had similar experiences with retaliation as those respondents in the more representative *RMWS*.

Across DoD surveys, most Service members give their senior unit leadership high marks in creating a climate that supports sexual assault reporting and does not penalize a victim for reporting. However, the *2014 SES* indicated that this highly favorable rating does not extend all the way down the chain of command. As a result, the Secretary of Defense directed in December 2014 that the Services were to create training for enlisted members and junior officers serving as first-line supervisors that helps them identify and prevent retaliation.

In order to better assess the experience of retaliation and identify potential points for intervention, the Department plans to conduct a systematic review of retaliation allegations made to the Service commands and Inspectors General. In addition, the Department will revise its survey questions to better align with Department policy and law addressing reprisal and ostracism. Also, the Department will follow up on installation case management group (CMG) execution of the Secretary's directive to inquire about allegations of retaliation during monthly meetings. These attempts to better define the scope of the problem and capture the efforts taken to address this unacceptable behavior will inform Department-wide efforts to prevent retaliation associated with reporting sexual assault.

Line of Effort 5: Assessment Programs and Initiatives

Assessment is an enduring process of data collection and analysis designed to improve program effectiveness and is embedded within the four other LOEs. The enhancements implemented in FY 2014 under the Assessment LOE aim to achieve the end state of incorporating responsive, meaningful, and accurate systems of measurement and evaluation into every aspect of the SAPR program.

Completed Assessment Strategic Plan Tasks

In FY 2014, the Department completed the following tasks presented in the *DoD SAPR Strategic Plan*:

- Implemented a dispositions and case synopsis module into the Defense Sexual Assault Incident Database (DSAID);
- Harmonized DoD and Services' survey methodologies, frequency, and key metrics to effectively standardize, measure, analyze, assess, and report program progress; and
- Oversaw the implementation of Defense Task Force on Sexual Assault in the Military Services recommendations.

Secretary of Defense Assessment Initiatives

Secretary of Defense Assessment Initiatives

	Action	Status
Elevate Oversight	Complete	●
Develop Standardized Voluntary Survey for Victims and Survivors	Complete	●

● Complete

In progress

✖ No Progress

Under the Assessment LOE, the Department's objective is to effectively standardize measure, analyze, assess, and report SAPR program successes. The actions taken in support of the Secretary of Defense Assessment initiatives help to ensure the overall effectiveness of the Department's SAPR program.

Elevate Oversight

In August 2013, the Secretary of Defense directed the USD(P&R) to develop policy, standardized across the Military Services, which requires status reports of unrestricted sexual assault allegations and actions taken to the first General Officer/Flag Officer (GO/FO) within the chain of command, without delaying reporting to the relevant MCIO. This was also required per the NDAA for FY 2014.[66] USD(P&R) issued DTM 14-007 outlining this requirement, titled "Sexual Assault Incident Report Oversight (SAIRO)" that was published in FY 2014. The status reports must be completed within 8 days of an Unrestricted Report via a DD Form 2910 or an initiation of an independent investigation of sexual assault by a MCIO. Although a SAIRO Report is not required for Restricted Reports, a SARC does inform his/her commander when an incident occurs without providing personally identifiable information (PII) of the victim or alleged offender.

The SAIRO Report is prepared by the assigned immediate commander with input from the SARC and MCIO, and submitted to the required O-6 or GO/FO as outlined in the SAIRO DTM. This oversight creates visibility and transparency of the response to victims for senior leaders and system accountability.

The Department continually seeks to improve DoD's response to victims and the SAIRO Report is another pathway to ensuring that victims receive the resources and support they deserve. The SAIRO Report assures that victims are offered healthcare, victim advocacy, timely investigation, safety assessments, notice of expedited transfers and military protective orders, and the legal services of a SVC/VLC. This initial report elevates oversight of the immediate response system elements.

Develop Standardized Voluntary Survey for Victims and Survivors

In FY 2014, the Chiefs of the Military Services and NGB were required to develop and participate in a standardized victim survey. This tool is to provide victims or survivors the opportunity to provide feedback on their experiences with SAPR victim assistance, the military health system, the military justice process, and other areas of support.

The *2014 SES* provided data included in the *Report to the President*. The purposes of the *SES* were to:

- Capture critical feedback on victim satisfaction and confidence in the system;
- Assess the impact of recent initiatives and policies on victims; and
- Meet the *Report to the President* requirement.

A more detailed explanation of the *SES* can be found in the *Report to the President* on page 125.

FY 2014 Assessment Programmatic Highlights

In addition to the Secretary of Defense initiatives, the Department implemented several other efforts in support of the Assessment LOE in FY 2014. This section provides highlights of the significant accomplishments.

Maintained and Refined DSAID

Defense Sexual Assault Incident Database (DSAID) captures case information input by the Military Service and NGB SARCs about both Restricted and Unrestricted Reports, enhances a SARC's ability to provide comprehensive and standardized victim case management, enables properly trained legal officers to input and validate case disposition data, supports Service SAPR program management, provides improved oversight of how sexual assault cases are managed, and enables the Department to meet Congressional reporting requirements.[67] DSAID may only be accessed by D-SAACP certified SARCs, Service legal officers, and SAPR Program Managers. In FY 2014, Army SARCs were brought into the system, making DSAID the common case management and reporting tool across the Department. At the request of the USCG, the Department is now working to integrate USCG SARCs into DSAID in FY 2015.

DSAID

DEFENSE SEXUAL ASSAULT INCIDENT DATABASE

Case Management | Business Management | Reporting

Figure 10. DSAID Logo.

Other enhancements to DSAID since FY 2013 include:

- Expanding expedited transfer functionality to capture more information and allow for the tracking of multiple transfers;
- Modifying functionality for SARCs to upload a scanned image of a DD Form 2910, *Victim Reporting Preference Statement,* for Unrestricted Reports, enhancing long-term availability of documentation to assist survivors in obtaining a record copy of the form;

- Implementing a reporting functionality for Service SAPR Program Managers to generate quarterly and annual Service reports, Military Service Academy (MSA) reports, and customized data queries; and
- Implementing a web-based, self-guided training solution for SARCs and SAPR Program Managers consisting of simulations of DSAID's capabilities.

Given the great interest in case outcome information, the Department created a centralized case disposition module to streamline capturing and reporting case outcomes across the Military Services. Implemented by the Department in FY 2014, this enhancement enables Service legal officers to validate subject case dispositions entered by SARCs, track subject case outcomes, and record subject punishment information, as applicable. The Department aggregates and analyzes this data to support Department metric and non-metric[68] information and inform SAPR policy. For the first time, DSAID provided the data to produce this Annual Report and will continue to do so in the future.

The Department certified DSAID for compliance with all security requirements and is accredited for operation by the Designated Approval Authority (DAA) Representative. SAPRO continues to enhance DSAID according to internal and external requirements, while collaborating with the system developer and the Military Services throughout the full system development lifecycle. Additional details on the Department efforts to continually enhance DSAID can be found on pages 123-125 of the *Report to the President.*

Responded to the GAO's Recommendations in "DoD Needs to Take Further Action to Prevent Sexual Assault during Initial Military Training"

In September 2014, the GAO released *DoD Needs to Take Further Action to Prevent Sexual Assault During Initial Military Training*. It concluded that DoD has taken a number of actions to prevent, investigate, and respond to sexual assault. However, recruits and other junior enlisted Service members appear to be especially vulnerable to sexual assault and related misconduct. The AF has been proactive in addressing how to improve the climate during basic training to prevent sexual assault since a number of allegations became known in 2012. Following these allegations, the AF completed an evaluation of the basic military training environment. This commander-directed investigation resulted in 46 specific action items for change in the basic military training environment.

According to the GAO, AF officials believe that their actions as a whole have improved the climate at basic training. However, GAO added that until the AF identifies a timeframe for establishing performance goals and measures to evaluate the effectiveness and improvements resulting from its actions taken, it will be unable to gauge its progress or take corrective actions when needed to address unforeseen problems that may arise or actions that are not working as intended. The AF provided an update on its actions to meet the recommendations from the GAO in its annual report, located at Enclosure 3 of this report.

Overarching Tenets

In addition to the five LOEs in the *DoD SAPR Strategic Plan,* two overarching tenets that intersect all LOEs are provided: Communications and Policy. These tenets are essential to refining a professional military culture and command climate and set conditions required to optimize program implementation.

Completed Overarching Tenet Strategic Plan Tasks

The tasks provided for the Communications Tenet are continual efforts that the Department sustains each fiscal year.[69] For the Policy Tenet, DoD completed the following tasks in FY 2014:

- Modified policy provisions for command climate assessments;
- Modified policy provisions for dissemination of sexual assault information (e.g., hotline phone numbers and internet websites);
- Modified policy provisions for general education campaign for correction of military records when victims experience retaliation;
- Modified policy for record of dispositions of Unrestricted Reports;
- Established policy to require GO/FO review of and concurrence with a recommendation to involuntarily separate a Service member who made an Unrestricted Report of sexual assault if the Service member requests a GO/FO review;
- Established policy for the use of DoD funds and facilities for pregnancy termination as an option in cases of rape and incest;

- Established/reinforced policies to ensure recruits convicted of sexual assault offenses do not receive accession waivers and to require mandatory processing for administrative separation of Service members convicted of committing a sexual assault, when their sentence does not include a punitive discharge.

Key Accomplishment: Established/Reinforced Policies Regarding Recruits Convicted of Sexual Assault Offenses

In FY 2014, the Services reviewed and established new policies, as necessary, to ensure recruits convicted of sexual assault offenses do not receive accession waivers and to require mandatory processing for administrative separation of Service members convicted of committing a sexual assault.

At DoD level, DoD Directive (DoDD) 6495.01, "Sexual Assault Prevention and Response Program;" DoDI 6495.02, "SAPR Program Procedures;" DoDI 1332.14, "Enlisted Administrative Separations;" and DoDI 1332.30, "Separation of Regular and Reserve Commissioned Officers" provide policy guidance to meet the objective of this task. DoDI 1332.14 and DoDI 1332.30 were both published in FY 2014.

DoDD 6495.01 states:

> Enlistment or commissioning of personnel in the Military Services shall be prohibited and no waivers are allowed when the person has a qualifying conviction (see Glossary) for a crime of sexual assault.[70]

DoDI 6495.02 states:

> DoD prohibits granting a waiver for commissioning or enlistment in the Military Services when the person has a qualifying conviction (see Glossary) for a crime of sexual assault or is required to be registered as a sex offender.

DoDI 1332.14 states:

> Prescribe internal procedures to ensure enlisted Service members who are convicted of a covered sexual offense and are not punitively discharged are processed for administrative separation in accordance with

section 572(a)(2) of Reference (c), as described in the procedures of this instruction.

DoDI 1332.30 states:

That any commissioned officer convicted of rape or sexual assault as defined in subsection (a) or (b) of section 920 of Reference (d), forcible sodomy as defined in section 925 of Reference (d), or an attempt to commit one of those offenses, and who is not punitively discharged for such a conviction, will be processed for administrative separation once the conviction is final, in accordance with section 572(a)(2) of Reference (c).

Key Accomplishment: Established Policy to Require GO/FO Review of an Involuntarily Separation of a Service Member Who Made an Unrestricted Report

In order to enhance victim protections, the Office of USD(P&R) published DoDI 1332.14 and DoDI 1332.30 in FY 2014, which require a GO/FO review of and concurrence with a recommendation to involuntarily separate a Service member who made an Unrestricted Report of sexual assault if the Service member requests a GO/FO review.

DoDI 1332.14 states:

An enlisted Service member who made an Unrestricted Report of sexual assault and who is recommended for involuntary separation from the Military Services within 1 year of final disposition of his or her sexual assault case may request a general or flag officer (G/FO) review of the circumstances of and grounds for the involuntary separation.

DoDI 1332.30 states:

A commissioned officer who made an Unrestricted Report of sexual assault and who is recommended for involuntary separation from military service within 1 year of final disposition of his or her sexual assault case may request a G/FO review of the circumstances of and grounds for the involuntary separation. This requirement expands the requirement of section 578 of Reference (c) to ensure that an involuntary separation is not initiated in retaliation for making an Unrestricted Report of sexual assault.

NDAA Requirement Implementation

The last three NDAAs focused significantly on SAPR issues with 71 sections of law containing more than 100 unique requirements, to include 16 congressional reporting requirements. The NDAA for FY 2014 includes 33 sections of law, representing more than 50 individual provisions pertaining to SAPR. It represents the most sweeping reform to the UCMJ since 1968, with 16 military justice provisions. The NDAA for FY 2014 mandates eight distinct reports to assure congressional oversight. Seven of the eight required congressional reports were submitted by the end of FY 2014. The final report on the recently commenced Judicial Proceedings Panel (section 1731 of the NDAA for FY 2014) is expected to be submitted by the panel in 2017.

Of the 41 Secretary of Defense initiatives since December 2011, 19 are now in law following the passage of the FY 2014 and prior NDAAs. The NDAA for FY 2014 alone codifies eight Secretary of Defense initiatives.

Implementation of these provisions is well underway with many provisions fully implemented. The initiatives and congressional requirements are also being incorporated in the revision of DoDI 6495.02, including Change 2.[71] The following highlights three provisions that the Department implemented from a comprehensive list of implemented NDAA for FY 2014 provisions:

- First, each of the Services have implemented regulations addressing retaliation, ostracism, and maltreatment of sexual assault victims, making these acts punishable under Article 92, UCMJ;[72]
- Second, the Department has issued policy requiring a SAIRO report be completed within 8 days of a sexual assault report. These oversight reports allow senior leaders visibility into the steps being taken to offer the victim medical and mental healthcare, advocacy, legal services, and to capture the progress of the initial investigation;
- Third, the Department also updated its document retention policy for the DD Form 2910, wherein victims document their reporting option, and the DD Form 2911, the SAFE report. This was the third change in document retention requirements since 2011, as the NDAAs for FY 2012 and FY 2013 also had their own requirements. Both forms are now automatically retained for 50 years, allowing victims to access their records for any lawful purpose, including their application for disability benefits and other assistance.

The Department remains committed to the effective and efficient implementation of the NDAA requirements.

WAY FORWARD IN FY 2015

This report and the *Report to the President* document considerable progress in FY 2014 and prior years to address sexual assault in the military. While there are positive indications that the many steps taken to prevent and respond to sexual assault are having desired effects, more must be done to eliminate the crime. In FY 2015, DoD will continue to work together with the Services to incorporate best practices and reforms that improve its ability to address this crime.

Implement the NDAA for FY 2015 Requirements

The NDAA for FY 2015 included further amendments to the UCMJ, which the Department will implement in FY 2015. Examples of these military justice provisions include:

- Section 532 – Modifying when depositions may be ordered;
- Section 533 - Codifying SVC representation for members of the Reserve and National Guard who are the victims of sex-related offenses;
- Section 534(b) - Ensuring that victims are consulted concerning their preference for prosecution by military or civilian authorities for offenses in the United States and that their preference is considered;
- Section 536 – Requiring the modifications of the military rules of evidence to produce "general military character" evidence of an accused is not admissible for purposes of showing the probability of innocence of the accused for certain specified offenses, including sexual assault; and
- Section 537 – Modifying the psychotherapist-patient privilege.

Update DoD Policy and Strategic Plan

Understanding the need for continuous improvement, the Department will release an update of DoDI 6495.02, "Sexual Assault Prevention and Response Program Procedures," and has already updated the *DoD SAPR Strategic Plan*. The updated DoDI 6495.02 will reflect requirements from the FY 2014 and prior NDAAs, as well as a number of RSP recommendations. The revised *DoD SAPR Strategic Plan,* released in January 2015, contains 50 new tasks based on NDAA for FY 2014 requirements, Secretary of Defense initiatives, and input from the SAPR IPT. Going forward, DoD SAPRO will continue to track the Department's progress implementing the Strategic Plan tasks.

Additional Secretary of Defense Initiatives

With the release of the *Report to the President*, Secretary Hagel issued additional initiatives to address some of the challenges identified in the *Report* that DoD will address in FY 2015. These initiatives are:

- Installation Prevention Project: To advance knowledge and understanding of successful intervention policies, the Secretaries of the Military Departments, the Chiefs of the Military Services and the USD(P&R) will conduct a multi-year initiative to customize prevention efforts at select military installations. This effort will identify installation and community risk factors for sexual assault and develop associated actions leadership can take to mitigate sexual violence.
- Enhance First Line Supervisor Skills and Knowledge: To further advance a climate of dignity and respect, and prevent the potential for retaliation associated with reporting, the Chiefs of the Military Services and the NGB will augment all supervisor training to address the role of the supervisor in unit sexual assault prevention and response programs. This training will apply to all junior officers, junior enlisted supervisors, and civilian employees who supervise military members. Curriculum will emphasize the importance of engaging with subordinates on sexual assault prevention and response, recognizing the signs of possible acts of retaliation, and provide the opportunity to practice leadership skills to promote a healthy command climate.

- Engage Command to Prevent Retaliation: To enhance victim safety and recovery, the Chiefs of the Military Services and the NGB will develop new procedures for installation commanders who serve as the SAPR CMG Chair. These procedures will require installation commanders to regularly assess, and refer for appropriate corrective action, all reports from a victim, witness, or first responder of retaliation, ostracism, maltreatment, or reprisal in conjunction with a report of sexual assault.
- Provide Feedback to the Force: To encourage greater victim reporting and demonstrate Department and Service progress, the Secretaries of the Military Departments will provide the findings in the *Report to the President* to all Service members in an interactive manner.

Operationalize the Prevention Strategy

In FY 2015, the Department will continue with the implementation of the *2014-2016 DoD Sexual Assault Prevention Strategy*. Efforts are focused on operationalizing the strategy to ensure Service members at every level of the Department have the knowledge and tools to prevent this crime. Given the importance of future leaders in ensuring an enduring solution, the Department will expand its efforts to target Junior Reserve Officer Training Corps and Reserve Officer Training Corps units to prepare them to address SAPR issues upon accession or commissioning. DoD SAPRO will expand its collaboration with universities and MSAs to share promising prevention practices.

Ongoing GAO Reports

In October 2013, GAO announced that it will be reviewing DoD's programs for male victims. Recently, the GAO concluded its review and presented six recommendations to improve DoD's SAPR services for male Service members. DoD is currently working with the GAO to better apply its data in ways that inform decision-makers about the needs of male victims, evaluate what men might need that is different from women in the form of treatment, enhance provider training, and improve messaging. The Department is committed to preventing sexual assault throughout the entire force and improving response services to meet the needs of both male and female Service members. Appendix C presents GAO's recommendations and discusses the progress the Department has already made in addressing the recommendations, as well as the Department's plans for future progress in this area.

In July 2014, GAO announced an additional review of DoD's SAPR program, specifically the Department's efforts to prevent sexual assault in the military. The GAO is examining how DoD developed its *2014-2016 Sexual Assault Prevention Strategy* and how it is being implemented. The GAO's final report and recommendations for DoD's prevention efforts will be published in FY 2015.

CONCLUSION

The actions taken in FY 2014 reflect DoD's ongoing commitment to preventing this crime, through a carefully constructed system of checks and balances that provide professional advocacy, independent investigations and legal analysis, command engagement to ensure safety and victim care, and cross functional oversight mechanisms, capabilities, and services that enable a comprehensive response to a report of sexual assault.

Despite a great deal of progress, more work needs to be done to combat sexual assault in the military. The Department remains focused on leveraging its culture and core values to continue a tradition consistent with society's highest expectations of its military's standards. Every Service member deserves a military where sexist behaviors, sexual harassment, and sexual assault are not tolerated, condoned, or ignored. To this end, leaders have the tools to assess and promote an appropriate command climate where sexual assault and other destructive behaviors are prevented, sexual assault reporting is encouraged, and victim support is unparalleled.

DoD continues to implement the RSP recommendations, Secretary of Defense initiatives, and NDAA requirements. Furthermore, the Secretary of Defense issued additional initiatives today. The Secretaries of the Military Departments, in collaboration with the Acting USD(P&R), will incorporate insights derived from the *2014 RMWS* into prevention training for sexual harassment, sexual assault, and reporting-related retaliation. Additionally, the Acting USD(P&R) will assess clinical interventions that address the specific needs of men and women who are seeking treatment for sexual assault. The Acting USD(P&R) will also conduct force-wide sexual assault and sexual harassment prevalence surveys biennially for the Military Services and National Guard, using the measures created for the *2014 RMWS*, consistent with title 10 U.S.C. section 481. In alternate years, focus groups will be conducted by the DMDC to obtain feedback from the field. To better respect Service member survey burden and privacy, all other entities within the DoD will refrain from conducting force-wide surveys for determining the prevalence of sexual assault and sexual harassment. The surveys and focus groups will be developed and conducted in collaboration with the Secretaries of the Military Departments, the Chiefs of the Military Services, and NGB. Finally, the Acting USD(P&R), in collaboration with the Secretaries of the Military Departments and the DoD IG, will establish a comprehensive strategy to prevent retaliation against Service members who report or intervene on behalf of the victim in instances of sexual assault and other crimes.

End Notes

[1] Department of Defense Directive 6495.01 defines sexual assault as intentional sexual contact characterized by use of force, threats, intimidation, or abuse of authority or when the victim does not or cannot consent. The crime of sexual assault includes a broad category of sexual offenses consisting of the following specific Uniform Code of Military Justice offenses: rape, sexual assault, aggravated sexual contact, abusive sexual contact, forcible sodomy (forced oral or anal sex), or attempts to commit these offenses.

[2] The use of the terms “victim” or “survivor” as they appear in this report are not intended to presume the commission of a crime or the guilt or innocence of any individual.

[3] The report also satisfies the following additional statutory reporting requirements: section 542 of Carl Levin and Howard P. “Buck” McKeon National Defense Authorization Act for Fiscal Year 2015 (Public Law 113-291); section 575 of National Defense Authorization Act for Fiscal Year 2013 (Public Law 112- 239); section 567 of National Defense Authorization Act for Fiscal Year 2010 (Public Law 111-84); and section 596 of National Defense Authorization Act for Fiscal Year 2006 (Public Law 109-163).

[4] The Department’s SAPR program is governed by Department of Defense Directive 6495.01, “Sexual Assault Prevention and Response Program,” and Department of Defense Instruction 6495.02, “Sexual Assault Prevention and Response Program Procedures.”

[5] Of 477,513 Department of Defense Active Duty Service members invited to take the survey, 145,300 participated (about 30%). The respondents included 34% of the women sampled and about 28% of the men sampled.

[6] The *Survivor Experience Survey* is an on-going survey of sexual assault survivors who volunteer to provide feedback on their experiences with the sexual assault response system. Data described in this report refer to a sample of 151 survivors who participated in the survey from June 4 to September 22, 2014. The results of the *Survivor Experience Survey* may not be representative of all survivors in the force.

[7] Each report consists of an official report documented by a Sexual Assault Response Coordinator and/or Military Criminal Investigative Organization of an allegation of adult sexual assault that falls under Uniform Code of Military Justice articles defining rape, sexual assault, aggravated sexual contact, abusive sexual contact, nonconsensual sodomy, and attempts of these crimes.

[8] Sexual assault is an underreported crime. This means the number of sexual assaults estimated to occur each year vastly outnumbers reports made to DoD authorities. While sexual assault remains underreported, the Department views increased reporting of the crime as beneficial for victims. Reporting allows victims to engage restorative care and services. In addition, it allows the Department to hold offenders appropriately accountable.

[9] An Unrestricted Report of sexual assault is a report that is provided to command and/or law enforcement for investigation.

[10] Restricted Reporting allows victims to confidentially access medical care and advocacy services without triggering an investigation. Victims may convert their Restricted Report to an Unrestricted Report at any time and participate in the military justice process.

[11] RAND Corporation used scientific weighting to estimate prevalence rates that were representative of the entire active duty population. Full methodological details and results are included in Annex 1.

[12] RAND Corporation administered two versions of the prevalence survey; the *Workplace and Gender Relations Survey* form used questions from past surveys to allow for historical comparison and the *RAND Military Workplace Study* form used questions more closely aligned with legal language. Unwanted sexual contact is the *Workplace and Gender Relations Survey* term for the range of sexual crimes between adults. Unwanted Sexual Contact involves intentional sexual contact that was against a person's will or occurred when the person did not or could not consent. The term describes completed and attempted oral, anal, and vaginal penetration with any body part or object, and the unwanted touching of genitalia and other sexually related areas of the body. "Sexual assault," instead of unwanted sexual contact, is used when referring to the *RAND Military Workplace Study* form because that version of the survey more closely aligns with legal language. Past-year prevalence rates described in this report are primarily drawn from the *Workplace and Gender Relations Survey* form.

[13] The decrease in prevalence for active duty men from 2012 to 2014 was not statistically significant.

[14] The *Workplace and Gender Relations Survey of Active Duty Members* is conducted every two years by the Department, as required by 10 United States Code Section 481. In 2013, the Secretary directed that the 2014 *Workplace and Gender Relations Survey of Active Duty Members* be conducted by an agency external to the Department. Therefore, RAND Corporation conducted the survey to determine the 2014 unwanted sexual contact prevalence rate.

[15] As with all victim surveys, RAND classifies service members as experiencing sexual assault, sexual harassment, or gender discrimination based on their memories of the event as expressed in their survey responses. It is likely that a full review of all evidence would reveal that some respondents whom RAND classifies as not having experienced sexual

assault, sexual harassment, or gender discrimination based on their survey responses actually did have one of these experiences. Similarly, some whom RAMD classifies as having experienced a crime or violation may have experienced an event that would not meet the minimum DoD criteria. A principal focus of RAND's survey development was to minimize both of these types of errors, but they cannot be completely eliminated in a self-report survey.

[16] Although 5,284 Service member victims made sexual assault reports in FY 2014, 516 of them made a report for events that occurred prior to their entry into military service. This leaves 4,768 victims who made a report for an incident that occurred during military service.

[17] This graph depicts the estimated number of Service members who experienced unwanted sexual contact in the past year (based on the *Workplace and Gender Relations Survey of Active Duty Members* estimated prevalence rates), versus the number of Service member victims in actual reports of sexual assault made to the Department in the years indicated. Note that although 5,284 Service members were victims and/or subjects in sexual assault reports in fiscal year 2014, 516 of them made a report for events that occurred prior to their entry into military service.

[18] It should be noted that the survey data collected provides broad perceptions of retaliation that do not necessarily align with actionable offenses that meet the elements of proof required for a charge of retaliation under military law.

[19] On the *2014 RAND Military Workplace Study*, RAND provided the following as examples of professional retaliation: loss of privileges, denied promotion/training, and transferred to less favorable job. RAND provided the following as examples of social retaliation: being ignored by coworkers and being blamed for the situation. Examples of adverse administrative actions on the *2014 RAND Military Workplace Study* included being placed on medical hold, placed on a legal hold, and transferred to a different assignment. On the survey, RAND provided the following as examples of infractions for which victims were cited: underage drinking or fraternization. Adverse administrative actions and punishment for infractions are not included under the category of "professional retaliation" because these actions are not necessarily retaliatory. They could occur after a sexual assault report to address victim safety and health concerns or to address collateral misconduct under military law. However, if these actions are taken with the intention of penalizing a victim for reporting a sexual assault, they could be considered professional retaliation.

[20] This was required by the Secretary of Defense in his memorandum that was published in December 2014. The memo can be found here: http://www.sapr.mil/public/docs/reports/FY14POTUS/FY14 DoD Report to POTUS SecDef Initiatives. pdf.

[21] Department of Defense Instruction 1304.33, "Protecting Against Inappropriate Relations During Recruiting and Entry Level Training," January 28, 2015.

[22] Section 1732 (2) In-progress. The Inspector General is developing uniform policy regarding case determinations.

[23] At the time of publishing this report, a total of 50 initiatives were directed by the Secretary of Defense. Thirty-five of the 50 have been completed, 4 are awaiting the Secretary's review, and 11 are in progress. These initiatives also include measures to be implemented by the Military Service Academies. The progress that the Military Service Academies have taken to implement the initiatives was discussed in the *Department of Defense Annual Report on Sexual Harassment and Violence at the Military Service Academies, Academic Program Year 2013-2014.*

[24] The use of the terms "offenders" or "perpetrators" as used in this report is not intended to make any suggestions or conclusions as to whether the commission of a crime occurred.

[25] The report satisfies the following statutory reporting requirements: section 542 of Carl Levin and Howard P. "Buck" McKeon NDAA for FY 2015 (Public Law (P.L.) 113-291); section 575 of NDAA for FY 2013 (P.L. 112-239); sections 1602 and 1631 of Ike Skelton NDAA for FY11 (P.L. 111-383); section 567 of NDAA for FY10 (P.L. 111-84); and section 596 of NDAA for FY06 (P.L. 109-163).

[26] Annual reports from 2004 to 2006 were based on the calendar year (CY); annual reports from 2007 to the present are based on the fiscal year (FY).

[27] DoDI 6495.02 requires a minimum of bi-monthly meetings. The SAPR IPT met more frequently than bimonthly during FY 2014.

[28] JCS's Strategic Direction to the Joint Force was issued in May 2012.

[29] Section 576 of the NDAA for FY 2013 was amended by the NDAA for FY 2014.

[30] GAO-14-806, "Military Personnel: DoD Needs to Take Further Actions to Prevent Sexual Assault During Initial Military Training," September 9, 2014 (GAO Code 351840). Available here: http://www.gao.gov/assets/670/665632.pdf.

[31] Harned, M.S., Ormerod, A.J., Palmieri, P.A., Collinsworth, L.L. & Reed, M. (2002). "Sexual assault and other types of sexual harassment by workplace personnel: a comparison of antecedents and consequences," *Journal of Occupational Health Psychology 7(2):* 174-88.

[32] USC is the *Workplace and Gender Relations Survey* proxy term for the crimes that constitute sexual assault under Department policy.

[33] The decrease in prevalence for active duty men from 2012 to 2014 was not statistically significant. The 2014 prevalence rates presented in this section were calculated by RAND Corporation using the "USC" measure from prior administrations of the *WGRA*, in order to provide an accurate comparison with previous rates. Additional information on the RAND study can be found in Annex 1.

[34] *2014-2016 DoD Sexual Assault Prevention Strategy*, April 30, 2014, can be found here: http://sapr.mil/index.php/prevention/prevention-strategy

[35] Section 1741 of the NDAA for FY 2014.

[36] The objective of the Prevention Roundtable is to establish a forum for communication in which participants share information on DoD sexual assault prevention efforts and requirements.

[37] The VLC is Navy's SVC program.

[38] The Special Victim Capability, described in prior Department materials has since been re-named the Special Victim Investigation and Prosecution (SVIP) capability so as not to be confused with the Special Victims' Counsel (SVC) program, which provides attorneys to represent the interests of victims of sexual assault in the military justice process.

[39] DoD IG found, in its report published on March 24, 2015, that nearly all adult sexual assault investigations were completed as required by guiding policies. Of 536 MCIO investigations, 532 (99%) met investigative standards or had only minor investigative and/or administrative deficiencies.

[40] The SVC program is discussed in the Accountability LOE.

[41] *Establishment of Special Victim Capabilities within the Military Departments to Respond to Allegations of Certain Special Victim Offenses* can be found here: http://www.sapr.mil/index.php/annual-reports.

[42] Please see page 10 of the *Establishment of Special Victim Capabilities within the Military Departments to Respond to Allegations of Certain Special Victim Offenses* report.

[43] The SVC program is discussed in the Accountability LOE section of this report.

[44] DTM 14-002 can be found here: http://www.sapr.mil/index.php/dod-policy/dod-and-service-policy. DTM 14-002 was superseded by DoDI 5505.19, "Establishment of SVIP Capability within the MCIOs," which was published on February 3, 2015.

[45] DTM 14-003 can be found here: http://www.sapr.mil/index.php/dod-policy/dod-and-service-policy.

[46] DODIG-2014-108, "Evaluation of Military Criminal Investigative Organizations' Adult Sexual Assault Investigation Policies," September 16, 2014. The full report is available here: http://www.dodig.mil/pubs/documents/DODIG-2014-108.pdf.

[47] Section 576 of the NDAA for FY 2013, as amended by the NDAA for FY 2014, directed the Secretary of Defense to establish the RSP "to conduct an independent review and assessment of the systems used to investigate, prosecute, and adjudicate crimes involving adult sexual assault and related offenses under section 920 of title 10, U.S.C. (Article 120 of the UCMJ), for the purpose of developing recommendations regarding how to improve the effectiveness of such systems."

[48] In addition to Accountability, Assess Military Justice System is an initiative that also falls within the Investigation and Victim Assistance/Advocacy LOEs.

[49] Section 1722 of the NDAA for FY 2014.

[50] The recommendation that was disapproved was to develop and implement policy that, when information comes to military police about an instance of sexual assault by whatever means, the first step in an investigation is to advise the victim that she or he has the right to speak with a special victim counsel before determining whether to file a Restricted or Unrestricted Report, or no report at all.

[51] Secretary of Defense memorandum, Subject: Department of Defense Implementation of the Recommendations of the Response Systems to Adult Sexual Assault Crimes Panel, December 15, 2014.

[52] The RSP report is available at www.responsesystempanel.whs.mil.

[53] This initiative is also a VA/Advocacy LOE effort.

[54] DODIG-2014-103, "Evaluation of DoD Compliance with the Sex Offender Registration and Notification Act," August 29, 2014. Full report is available here: http://www.dodig.mil/pubs/documents/DODIG-2014- 103.pdf.

[55] MRE 514, (a), "General Rule of Privilege."

[56] In FY 2015, the Department forwarded a recommendation to the President on relevant changes for the MCM.

[57] Section 1706 of the NDAA for FY 2014 imposed a similar requirement.

[58] Section 1713 of the NDAA for FY 2014.

[59] Section 1723 of the NDAA for FY 2014.

[60] The DoD Safe Helpline is located here: https://www.safehelpline.org/.

[61] The DoD Safe Helpline is an anonymous and confidential service and does not collect information that identifies any of its users.

[62] See generally Section 1709 of the NDAA for FY 2014.

[63] The *DEOCS* includes an opportunity for members of the Armed Forces to express their opinions regarding the manner and extent to which their leaders, including commanders, handle organization, equal opportunity, and equal employment opportunity issues within a unit.

[64] On the *2014 RAND Military Workplace Study,* RAND provided the following as examples of professional retaliation: loss of privileges, denied promotion/training, and transferred to less favorable job. RAND provided the following as examples of social retaliation: being ignored by coworkers and being blamed for the situation. Examples of adverse administrative actions on the *2014 RAND Military Workplace Study* included being placed on medical hold, placed on a legal hold, and transferred to a different assignment. Examples of infractions for which victims were cited included underage drinking or fraternization.

[65] The *SES* is also discussed in the Assessment LOE section of this report.

[66] Section 1743 of the NDAA for FY 2014.

[67] P.L. 110-417, Section 563 (a) and (d).

[68] "Non-metrics" are items that address the military justice process. There will be no effort to affect these aspects or outcomes, as doing so may constitute illegal command influence on military justice. However, given the substantive interest in the military justice system and how it functions, these items will be used to describe or illustrate certain aspects of the system.

[69] Please see page16 of the *DoD SAPR Strategic Plan* for a complete listing of the Communications tasks.

[70] DoDD 6495.01, "SAPR Program," Incorporating Change 1, April 30, 2013. 32 CFR Part 103 Final Rule (RIN 0790-AI37). Available at: http://www.sapr.mil/index.php/dod-policy/directives-and-instructions.

[71] Sec. 1732 (2) of the NDAA for FY 2014 In-progress. IG developing uniform policy regarding case determinations.

[72] While evidence of these acts may be punishable under military law, the Department recognized that there may be instances where the behavior falls short of the evidentiary requirements for military justice proceedings but require attention nonetheless. In January 2015, the Secretary of Defense directed DoD OGC, DoD IG, and the Secretaries of the Military Departments to conduct a comprehensive review of the means available to address both social and professional retaliation, to include appropriate social media conduct.

INDEX

A

B

C

D